‹SPAIN›

MAJOR WORLD NATIONS

SPAIN

Arthur Miller

CHELSEA HOUSE PUBLISHERS
Philadelphia

Chelsea House Publishers

Contributing Author: Joseph Barron

Copyright © 1999 by Chelsea House Publishers,
a division of Main Line Book Co.
All rights reserved.
Printed and bound in the United States of America.

First Printing

1   3   5   7   9   8   6   4   2

Library of Congress Cataloging-in-Publication Data

Miller, Arthur, 1924–
Spain.
Includes index.

Summary: Surveys the history, topography, people, and culture of Spain,
with emphasis on its current economy, industry, and place in the political
world.

1. Spain—juvenile literature. [1. Spain] I. Title
DP17.M65   1988   946.083   87-18326
ISBN-0-7910-4767-9

‹CONTENTS›

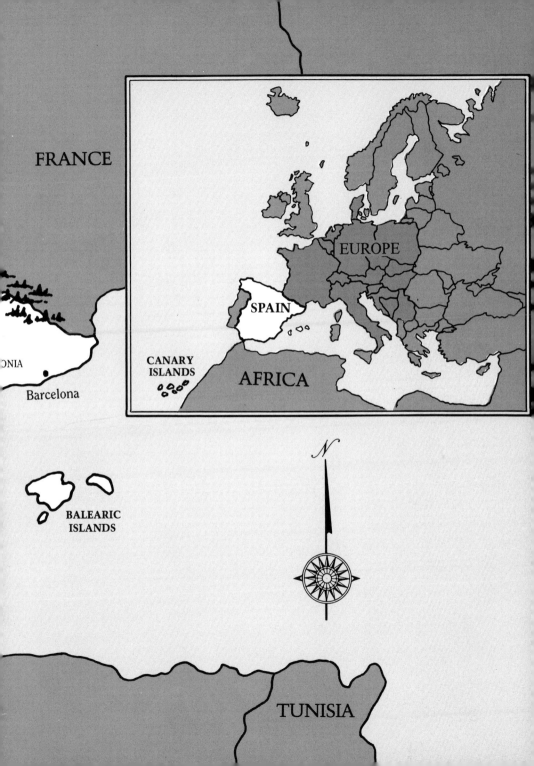

◄ FACTS AT A GLANCE ►

LAND AND PEOPLE

Area	195,000 square miles (505,000 square kilometers)
Highest Point	Mulhacén (continental)—11,400 feet (3,474 meters), Pico de Teide (in Canaries)—12,195 feet (3,717 meters)
Population	39,200,000
Population Density	202 per square mile (78 per square kilometer)
Capital	Madrid (population 3,085,000)
Other Major Cities	Barcelona (1,681,000); Valencia (777,000); Seville (705,000); Zaragoza (622,000); Bilbao (372,000)
Ethnic Groups	Spanish (Castilian, Valencian, Andalusian, Asturian)—74 percent; Catalan—17 percent; Galician—7 percent; Basque—2 percent
Languages	Castilian Spanish, Catalan, Galician, Basque
Religions	Roman Catholic—95 percent; other (Protestant, Jewish, Muslim), 5 percent

ECONOMY

Major Products	Iron and steel products, automobiles, machinery, ships, textiles, fruits and vegetables, footwear
Major Resources	Mercury, potash, uranium, copper, lead, iron, zinc, coal, cork
Labor Force	Agriculture—9 percent; industry and construction—30 percent; services—61 percent

Gross National Product (1995)	$565 billion U.S.
Currency	Peseta (1996, 127 pesetas = $1.00 U.S.)
Per Capita Income (1995)	$14,300 U.S.

GOVERNMENT

Form of Government	Parliamentary monarchy with two legislative houses (Senate and Congress of Deputies), together called the Cortes Generales. Seventeen regional subdivisions, called autonomous communities, each with a regional government and a parliament elected by universal vote. The nation adopted a democratic constitution in 1978.
Formal Head of State	King Juan Carlos I
Head of Government	Prime Minister José María Aznar
Eligibility to Vote	All those 18 years of age or older

◄HISTORY AT A GLANCE►

15,000–12,000 B.C.	Cave paintings at Altamira are created by prehistoric cultures.
3000 B.C.	Iberians settle the peninsula.
1000 B.C.	Celts cross the Pyrenees Mountains and settle in northern Spain; Phoenicians arrive from the eastern Mediterranean.
600s B.C.	Greek traders settle along the Mediterranean coast.
400s B.C.	Carthaginians arrive from northern Africa and conquer much of Spain.
200s B.C.	Roman forces drive Carthaginians from Spain and add the peninsula to their growing empire. The Romans introduce the Latin language and, later, Christianity.
400s A.D.	The Visigoths, Germanic tribes from Europe, take control of the Iberian Peninsula.
587	Catholicism is adopted as Spain's official religion.
711–718	Muslims (Moors) from northern Africa invade and conquer most of Spain.
700s–1400s	Christian forces reconquer Spain.
1478	The Spanish Inquisition begins.
1479	The kingdoms of Aragón and Castile unite, bringing all Spain under one crown.
1492	Christian troops defeat Moors at Granada, the last center of Moorish control in Spain; Christopher Columbus claims America for Spain.

1530–1680	Spain enjoys a Golden Age of exploration and cultural and artistic flowering. At its height the Spanish Empire includes Mexico, Central America, much of western North and South America, the West Indies, parts of Europe, and the Philippine Islands.
1588	The English navy defeats the Spanish Armada.
1700	The French Duke Philip of Anjou becomes King Philip V of Spain, initiating rule by the Bourbon dynasty of France.
1808	The French emperor Napoleon conquers Spain.
1813	Combined forces from Great Britain, Portugal, and Spain drive the French from Spain in the Peninsular War.

Tourists from all parts of the world flock to Spain's history-laden shores throughout the year. Tourism employs 10% of all workers.

1873–1874	Spain is governed by the First Republic.
1874–1931	The Bourbon family is restored to the throne.
1898	As a result of the Spanish-American War, Spain cedes Puerto Rico, the Philippine Islands, and Guam to the United States.
1931	In national elections, Spaniards vote overwhelmingly for a republican form of government. The Second Republic is established.
1936–1939	The Spanish Civil War breaks out; General Francisco Franco wins and becomes dictator of Spain.
1939–1945	Spain remains officially neutral in World War II, but provides assistance to Hitler of Germany and Mussolini of Italy.
1955	Spain is admitted to the United Nations.
1975	Franco dies; Prince Juan Carlos de Borbón becomes king of Spain.
1978	Spain adopts a new democratic constitution.
1982	Spain joins NATO. In elections, the Socialist party gains control of the government.
1983	A process of decentralization, begun in 1979, is completed, forming Spain's 17 autonomous communities.
1986	Spain joins the European Economic Community (now the European Union).
1996	In the general elections a coalition of conservative and regional parties wins control of the government, ending the 14-year rule of the Socialists.

Madrid, the capital city, is an exciting mixture of the new and the traditional.

Spain and the World

Spain lies at the southwestern corner of Europe, where it shares the Iberian Peninsula with Portugal. It is a mountainous country of high plateaus and narrow coastal plains, with bright sunlight and brilliant skies that have entranced artists and visitors alike. At its southern tip, Spain is separated by only a few miles of water from northern Africa, a region whose culture has exerted a strong influence on the country's history. Spain's total area, approximately 195,000 square miles (505,000 square kilometers), makes it Europe's third-largest nation—about the size of the states of Colorado and Utah combined.

Spain's early development was dictated by settlement and invasion by people from distant lands. Ancient ruins, towering castles, and magnificent churches are vivid reminders of the cultural diversity that resulted from this settlement. After the country was unified under one crown in the 15th century, Spain's rulers began an active overseas campaign of their own, opening the way for the most glorious chapter in the country's history—its Golden Age. Led by brave explorers who sailed into uncharted seas, Spain assembled an empire that was more vast than the realms of ancient Rome or 19th-century Great Britain. Spanish *conquistadores* (conquerors) carried their language, culture, and Catholic religion to Central and South America and the Philippine Islands and brought home vast riches.

Spain's role as a world power was short-lived, but the legacy of empire has endured: Over 400 million people throughout the world speak Spanish, and much of contemporary culture in these Spanish-speaking countries has its roots in Spanish colonization. More recently, Spain emerged from four decades of dictatorship when Francisco Franco died in 1975. Franco had ruled the country since 1939, when he emerged victorious after the Spanish Civil War. Franco was succeeded by King Juan Carlos I, who established a constitutional monarchy, bringing democracy to Spain at last.

Many people think of Spain as a land of bullfights, castles, and *senoritas* swirling in a flamenco dance. These remnants of old Spain still exist, but today a Spaniard is more likely to attend a soccer match than a bullfight, to vacation in a high-rise apartment instead of in a castle, and to dance at a disco instead of to the twang of a guitar.

Following the Spanish Civil War, Francisco Franco ruled as Spain's dictator for nearly 40 years.

However, Spain's traditional regional differences remain strong. More than almost any other country in Europe, Spain retains important cultural distinctions between its many regions, which were settled by diverse peoples and developed under the influence of vastly different factors. Today, many inhabitants identify first with their particular region, and then with the mother country. This fierce regional independence is reflected in the work of Spain's painters, writers, and architects; some regions even have their own languages, which inhabitants speak instead of the Castilian Spanish that is the official language of Spain.

The challenge for Spain's young democracy will be to find a way to blend the country's rich diversity with the need for the individualistic Spaniards to accept the discipline of a central government. A successful step toward this goal was taken in 1978, when the government legitimized Spain's regional diversity by allowing the regions to group together into 17 "autonomous communities," each with the power to elect its own parliament.

With political change has come economic change. One of the least-developed countries in Europe at the end of World War II, Spain has industrialized rapidly. Young Spaniards who not long ago might have remained in their villages to farm now head for jobs in city factories. In addition, the nation—once virtually isolated from the rest of Europe—has recently been accepted into various international organizations, including the United Nations, the Council of Europe, and the European Economic Community (EEC), now known as the European Union (EU). Since 1982, Spain has been a member of the North Atlantic Treaty Organization (NATO, a mutual defense organization), and it allows the alliance's aircraft and ships to operate from several bases on its territory. Spain also maintains close diplomatic and cultural ties with the countries of Latin America, most of which were first settled by Spaniards.

The Costa Brava, or "rugged coast," in northeastern Spain is a string of sheltered coves edged by beaches and small fishing villages.

Dry Plateau, Fertile Fringe

Spain occupies 85 percent of the Iberian Peninsula, located at the southwestern end of Europe. At its northern border, the Pyrenees Mountains form a natural barrier between Spain and France. Portugal and the Atlantic Ocean form Spain's western boundary, and the Mediterranean Sea forms its eastern and southeastern coastline, narrowing at Spain's southern tip to the tiny Strait of Gibraltar, which separates Spain from North Africa.

In addition to the country itself, which is called continental Spain, the nation also includes two island groups: the Balearics, off Spain's Mediterranean coast, and the Canary Islands, in the Atlantic off the northwest coast of Africa. Spain also retains two territories on the northern tip of Africa, the cities of Ceuta and Melilla. The total area of continental Spain and its islands and territorial holdings is approximately 195,000 square miles (505,000 square kilometers).

The dominant feature of continental Spain is a central plateau, called the *meseta*, which lies an average of 2,000 feet (610 meters) above sea level and covers about two-thirds of Spain's total area. The meseta extends from the Cantabrian Mountains in northern Spain to the Sierra Morena chain in the south. East of the meseta lie fertile plains that slope toward the Mediterranean Sea.

During the summer, warm air masses from Africa drift northward across the peninsula and are trapped by the Pyrenees Mountains chain along Spain's northern border. The warm air settles over the meseta, producing long, hot summers. The red and yellow soil turns dusty in the hot weather, and because of the scant rainfall on this high plateau only shrubs and a few flowering plants are able to grow. Winter brings the opposite extreme, as cold winds whistle across the open land.

The arid meseta provided the setting for the once-powerful Kingdom of Castile, one of many Christian kingdoms that fought amongst themselves between 1000 and 1400 A.D. Miguel de Cervantes portrayed the meseta in his classic 17th-century novel *Don Quixote*. As in Quixote's day, shepherds still herd their sheep and goats across the plateau, but their number is dwindling. Four of Spain's 17 autonomous communities (political subdivisions similar to states in the United States) are in this region. They are Castile-León, Castile-La Mancha, Madrid, and Extremadura. Madrid, also the nation's capital and largest city, is the chief commercial, cultural, and industrial city of the meseta.

Green, forested lands line Spain's northernmost regions. The northwest is known as "wet Spain," as opposed to the "dry Spain" of the meseta; in this terrain, the green color of forests and fields replaces the tan color of the plateau. Swift streams plunge through mountain gorges; apples grow in extensive orchards; bears and wolves roam the upland forests, and cattle graze in valley pastures. The autonomous communities of Galicia, Asturias, Cantabria, Basque Country, and Rioja occupy this section of the country.

In the northeast quarter of the country is the Ebro River valley, which is bordered by the Pyrenees Mountains to the north and the meseta to the west and south. The Ebro, Spain's second longest river, flows east 565 miles (911 km) from the northern mountains out into the Mediterranean. Farmers divert the river's water into irrigation ditches for their crops of wheat and orchards of peaches. The autonomous communities of Navarre, Aragón, and Catalonia are in this region. Zaragoza, in Aragón, is the region's main market city. Bustling Barcelona, Spain's busiest industrial city and port, is the major city of Catalonia and Spain's second-largest metropolis.

The plain that runs along Spain's Mediterranean coast, occupied by the autonomous communities of Valencia and Murcia, has a temperate climate that draws crowds of Europeans and Americans each year. This eastern coastal zone is the citrus- and rice-growing region of Spain and is one of the most intensely cultivated areas in Europe. Farmers use irrigation to supplement the sparse rainfall, producing harvests of citrus fruit to be shipped to world markets from the port city of Valencia. Valencia is Spain's third-largest city and shares its name with the autonomous community.

Southern Spain is dominated by the Guadalquivir River valley, where farmers grow the olives and grapes that are the country's two most valu-

The fertile pastures of Asturias lie between the Bay of Biscay and the Cantabrian Mountains, which contain much of Spain's coal deposits.

able crops; both were introduced to Spain by early Greek settlers. Pure-bred horses and fighting bulls are raised on the large estates that stretch across the rolling terrain of the autonomous community of Andalusia. The Guadalquivir, Spain's only navigable river, leads to the major port city of Seville, 60 miles upriver from the Atlantic Ocean. During the 16th and 17th centuries—Spain's Golden Age, when the country had conquered vast overseas possessions—galleons overflowing with gold and precious gems from the New World discharged their valuable cargoes at Seville.

Rivers

Three other major rivers rise in the central part of the meseta, flow west-ward through Extremadura and Castile-León, and reach the Atlantic Ocean through Portugal. They are, from north to south, the Douro, the Tagus (Spain's longest river, with a length of 625 miles, or approxi-mately 1000 kilometers), and the Guadiana. The Miño flows through Spain's northwest regions into the Atlantic; the Ebro River, located in northeastern Spain, flows from the Cantabrian Mountains east into the Mediterranean.

Mountains

Much of Spain is mountainous terrain; of all the European countries, Spain ranks second only to Switzerland in the average height of its land. Most of Spain's mountain ranges run east to west, and they include some of the highest peaks found in Europe: Mulhacén, in the Sierra Nevada range of southern Spain, is approximately 11,400 feet (3,474 meters) high, making it the highest point in continental Spain. (The country's highest point is Pico de Teide, on the island of Tenerife in the Canaries, at 12,195 feet or 3,717 meters.)

Vegetation and Animal Life

At one time, a large portion of Spain was covered by forests. In recent years, however, the use of trees for firewood, ship construction, and agriculture has greatly reduced the forest area. Deciduous trees (those whose leaves fall off in the winter and grow again in the spring) are common in the northern section of the country, where plentiful rainfall encourages oak, beech, ash, birch, and chestnut trees. In the arid regions, evergreens (those that keep their foliage year-round) such as pines and scrub types— also found in similar areas of northern Africa—predominate. Palm trees, oleanders, myrtles, poplars, and colorful bougainvilleas thrive in the temperate climate along the Mediterranean coast. Also found in this area are cork oak trees; the cork, stripped from the trees and exported to other countries, is an important Spanish product.

Among the wild animals that roam Spain's wilderness areas are goats, boars, wolves, foxes, deer, rabbits, and hares. The wild bird population includes storks, eagles, and vultures; partridge and quail are hunted as game birds.

The Balearic Islands and the Canary Islands have been sovereign parts of Spain for more than five centuries, and each is governed today as an autonomous community. The Balearic group, in the Mediterranean, consists of three major islands and several smaller ones. Their 1,936-square-mile (5,014-square-kilometer) area is characterized by rugged coastlines, lush vegetation, and a mild climate. The largest island, Mallorca (pronounced May-OR-ka), has an area of 1,405 square miles (3,639 sq km) and is home to the capital city of the Balearics, Palma de Mallorca. Grapes, olives, grapefruit, and other fruits flourish on the islands, and tourists from all over Europe make the tropical Balearics a popular destination during Europe's cold winter months.

The Canary Islands lie off the northwest coast of Africa, 800 miles (1,290 kilometers) southwest of Spain, and have belonged to Spain since 1479. This island group, with a total area of 2,808 square miles (7,273 sq km), is volcanic in origin. Its highest peak, Pico de Teide—at 12,195 feet (3,717 meters) high—is the highest mountain anywhere in Spain. The mountains slope down to fertile terrain where farmers cultivate large plantations of bananas and grow a variety of vegetables, fruits, and grains.

The meseta, a large, arid plateau, is in Spain's "dry section."

Some farmers still use camels as draft animals, a reminder that the Canaries lie close to Africa. The mild year-round climate that helps the crops thrive also attracts thousands of tourists who vacation each year on the two main islands of Grand Canary and Tenerife. Rainfall is scarce; water is carefully stored in cisterns in the mountains and flows through irrigation pipes to the fields below.

At the southernmost tip of Spain stands the rock of Gibraltar, a British colony whose fortified military base has long controlled sea traffic into and out of the Mediterranean. Gibraltar belonged to Spain until it was ceded to Britain in 1704. The famous rock functioned as an important military strongpoint for the Allies in both World Wars I and II. Since the mid-1980s, when Spain joined both the European Economic Community (EEC) and NATO, Britain has considered transferring sovereignty over Gibraltar to Spain. To encourage such negotiations, Spain has reopened its borders with Gibraltar to allow Spaniards access to the British colony.

In the first millennium B.C., the Phoenicians sailed to southern Spain from the eastern Mediterranean and set up trading posts.

Tides of History

Prehistoric humans entered the Iberian Peninsula from Africa approximately one million to 500,000 years ago. Between 15,000 and 12,000 B.C., a flourishing hunting culture existed in central and southern France and northern Spain. Spain's early inhabitants left a remarkable record of their activities: On the walls of caves such as the ones at Altamira, in Santander in northern Spain, these early humans painted pictures of bison, bulls, horses, goats, wild boars, and mammoths—the animals they hunted. These amazing paintings, created thousands of years ago, are still clear and bright today, although careful measures have been taken to protect them from air pollution and souvenir-hunters.

In approximately 3000 B.C., the Iberians, a people from northern Africa, began settling in southern and eastern Spain. The Iberians moved up the peninsula, ultimately establishing a tribal culture around the Ebro River valley in northeastern Spain. They developed an active pottery trade and engaged in agriculture and mining, using metals such as copper, iron, and bronze (a combination of copper and tin) to make weapons, utensils, and animal figurines. They also gathered in settlements to farm and to domesticate cattle.

During the first millennium B.C., the Celts, a race from northern Europe, drifted across the Pyrenees into northern Spain and mingled with the Iberians. Many of the Celts had blond hair and blue eyes; their legacy can be seen in northern Spain today, where many people have light colored eyes and fair skin and hair. In fact, the shading of people's hair and eyes grows progressively darker from northern Spain southward.

During the same era, the Phoenicians, a people from the far eastern end of the Mediterranean, reached southern Spain and set up trading posts. Expert sailors, the Phoenicians opened the entire Mediterranean to commerce and bartered with the Iberians for their agricultural crops and handsome metalwork. Two of their trading posts grew into the present-day cities of Cádiz and Málaga.

Greek settlers landed in Spain about 600 B.C. and established trading posts along the Mediterranean coast of eastern and southern Spain. They were soon followed by powerful military forces from Carthage, a Phoenician city state in northern Africa. The dominant power in the western Mediterranean, Carthage controlled the entire northern coast of Africa and soon took over southern Spain, confining the Greeks to the eastern coast. It is possible that the name "Spain" is derived from the Carthaginian word "spans" or "spania," meaning "land of the rabbits."

As their influence spread northward, the Carthaginians clashed with forces from Rome, who had recently arrived on the Iberian Peninsula. In 220 B.C., during the second of a series of three wars between Carthage and Rome, Hannibal, a prominent Carthaginian general, attacked and subdued the Spanish city of Saguntum, a Roman ally, and went on to lead the Carthaginian army in a trek across the Alps to attack the Romans in Italy. After a 15-year fight, Hannibal's campaign failed to subdue the Romans in their Italian homeland; in the meantime, Roman forces attacked and defeated the Carthaginians in Spain. By 205 B.C., Rome had taken control of Spain.

Spain Becomes a Roman Province

After overcoming the Carthaginians, the Roman legions had to subdue a number of independent tribes that inhabited the isolated valleys of the

Iberian Peninsula. It took them fully two centuries to accomplish this task. One city, Numantia, withstood 20 years of siege before surrendering.

The Romans called their new territory "Hispania," and it became part of an expanding Roman Empire that would grow to include the lands surrounding the Mediterranean and most of Europe. From their new colony the Romans extracted lead, silver, iron ore, tin, and gold. The soil and the sunny climate of southern Hispania produced crops of wheat, olives, and peppers. Horses raised in Spanish pastures pulled Roman chariots. Honey, wax, and other products were shipped back to Rome in the holds of the merchant ships that sailed regularly between Spain and Italy.

The Romans brought with them a sophisticated system of law and order, a blueprint for local government, and their language, Latin. Through force of arms, they consolidated the numerous settlements of Spain for the first time under one government. Towns developed as centers of commerce and government authority. After a time, the Spanish people gained the right to become Roman citizens and thereby to have certain rights, duties, and privileges. When Rome embraced Christianity as its official religion in the 4th century A.D., it introduced a religion that would form a central theme in Spain's history from that time on.

The conquerors also brought highly developed engineering skills to Spain. Roman engineers built roads and bridges to move troops about their vast empire, connect towns, and transport minerals and crops to the coast for export. Messengers on horseback galloped over the roads, bringing the latest news of the empire. The engineers also built stone aqueducts to transport water from mountain streams to the towns and farmers' fields. One such masterpiece, a magnificent 128-arch aqueduct that dates from the second century A.D. is still in use near Segovia, in central Spain.

As Roman influence spread over the peninsula, new towns were built on the plains and people moved out of mountain villages to populate them. Temples and buildings were erected for public feasts. Overseers built villas for themselves and decorated them with ornate mosaics. Spain today is a living museum of the remnants of these Roman towns and

Roman engineers built huge stone aqueducts to transport water from the mountains to the towns and to irrigate fields.

walled cities. At Itálica, near Seville, for example, stands a well-preserved amphitheater; at Tarragona is another aqueduct; and at Sagunto, near Valencia, are remains of the walled city of Avila.

The southern regions formed the cultural center of Romanized Spain. As local languages faded away by the first century A.D., Latin became Spain's official language. (Latin provided the basis for modern Romance languages such as French and Spanish, which would later spread halfway around the world.) A literature developed, and Spain produced such outstanding authors as Martial and Seneca. The arts flourished, with writers, sculptors, and painters working at several Spanish cities. Several of the greatest Roman emperors came from Spain as well, including Hadrian and Trajan, the first two emperors of Rome to be elected from outside Italy.

As a result of Roman rule, the Iberian Peninsula sustained three centuries of peace and order and its inhabitants enjoyed a time of relative prosperity. Then, however, the Spanish people fell prey to new invaders.

Visigothic Spain

Around 400 A.D., Germanic tribes from central Europe who had already overrun much of the civilized world began to intrude into Spain. The Vandal and Suebi peoples crossed the Pyrenees and settled in the northwest of Spain in what is now Galicia. Other Vandal tribes moved into southern Spain, where they gave their name to "Vandalusia," later short-

At the end of the 5th century, the Visigoths invaded and conquered Spain.

ened to "Andalusia." By the end of the 5th century, the Visigoths, another tribe, had defeated the others and gained control of the entire Iberian Peninsula.

The Visigoths chose to live in relative harmony with the conquered Hispanic people and showed their tolerance by allowing the natives to keep the ranks of nobility and social class distinctions they had acquired during Roman rule. The Visigoths even adopted many of the Roman ways: They spoke Latin, imitated the Romans in dress, adopted Roman laws, and preserved the Roman Catholic religion.

Moorish architects used floral and geometric designs to decorate their buildings.

Despite their initial success in their newly conquered lands, however, the Visigothic rulers lacked the organizational skills of their predecessors, and their kingdom gradually disintegrated as warring factions competed for control. In 711 A.D., the kingdom finally met its demise at the hands of Arab forces from North Africa.

Moors Bring a New Culture

The conquering Arab forces—Muslims, or Moors, as the Spanish called them—were followers of Muhammad, the founder of Islam, a new religion that had rapidly spread throughout the Middle East, northern Africa, and parts of Asia. By 718 A.D., the Moors, driven by a fierce religious zeal, occupied all of Spain except for the far valleys of the north.

The Muslim conquerors had learned much from the Greeks, Romans, Jews, and Christians as they swept along the shores of the Mediterranean, and they now shared their knowledge of mathematics, medicine, astronomy, philosophy, and other fields of study with the Spanish people. The Moors introduced new agricultural technology, extending the Roman irrigation system by building carefully engineered ditches and using waterwheels to produce power. From Africa they introduced new crops, including pomegranates, oranges, figs, dates, rice, sugarcane, and cotton. They brought many new musical instruments, including the lute and the oval guitar; they made fine glassware and pottery; they introduced paper and made possible the development of printing. They also founded Spain's first universities.

Like the Visigoths before them, the Moors were somewhat tolerant in matters of religion. Under their rule the cities of Spain had separate communities of Christians, Jews, and Muslims (Spain's Muslim population at this time included many Spanish people who had converted to Islam). Three cities grew and prospered one after another under Moorish rule. In the 900s, Córdoba, Spain's capital under Moorish rule, became the largest, wealthiest, and most civilized city in western Europe. Later, Moorish influence centered on Seville, then on Granada. In all three cities, Moorish architects constructed notable buildings, including beautiful mosques (Muslim places of worship), fortified palaces called *alcázars*, libraries, and schools.

Muslim designers decorated their architectural gems with large reflecting pools and fountains. Because the Koran, the holy book of Islam, prohibits the representation of the human figure, Muslim architects and artists used geometric and floral designs to decorate their buildings. These patterns are called "arabesques," because of their origins in the Arab world, and are reflected today in contemporary Spanish ceramics and carpets.

Many exquisite examples of Moorish architecture remain in Spain. The Grand Mosque at Córdoba is so huge that 850 columns are needed to support its dome. The Giralda, a minaret (religious tower) in Seville, was used to summon faithful Muslims to prayer. The Alhambra, an ornate palace that dominates the skyline of Granada, was the palatial dwelling of the Moorish kings. Today it provides a magnificent setting each summer for the annual Granada International Festival of Music and Dance that draws dancers, musicians, and orchestras from all over the world.

Christopher Columbus's voyages of exploration were financed by the Spanish monarchs Ferdinand and Isabella.

Golden Empire

When the Moors invaded Spain, a number of Christians fled and took refuge in the far northern regions. From this stronghold, they launched a series of attacks, collectively called the Reconquista (reconquest), in an effort to win their country back from the Arab invaders and restore the Visigoth monarchy.

As the Christian fighters pushed southward against the occupying Moors, they gathered strength from their own religious beliefs. They relied on a special protector, St. James the Great, who had preached Christianity in the north of Spain and then returned to Jerusalem, where he was beheaded. His body, legend said, was brought back to Spain and buried at Santiago de Compostela, in Galicia, where a large church was later erected in his honor. Many devout Christians made pilgrimages to the shrine throughout the Reconquista, and Christian soldiers marched to battle believing in St. James as their patron saint.

As Christian forces battled their way southward, they formed kingdoms and built castles to protect their newly won territory. The first kingdom, Asturias, was soon joined by other kingdoms as the Christian forces captured new land. By 1100, five Christian kingdoms—León (which had absorbed Asturias), Navarre, Aragón, Catalonia, and Castile—controlled most of the northern part of the peninsula. Castile, whose name is derived from the castles built to fortify the Christian territory, was located in the north-central part of the country and grew to be the strongest of the kingdoms, leading the fight for reconquest.

Each Christian kingdom developed a nobility based on military achievement. Kings rewarded their nobles with large tracts of land in appreciation for their military assistance, and young men from wealthy families became knights, called *infanzones* or *hidalgos*. The knights lived for the force of arms, fighting the king's battles, displaying their martial arts at fairs, and forming a close-knit chivalric brotherhood. Their fighting spirit was celebrated in a famous ballad, *The Poem of El Cid*, which tells of a Castilian knight who became one of Spain's national heroes after his heroic exploits against the Moors. El Cid won many battles and in 1094 won Valencia from the Moors. He became the symbol of Spanish resistance during the Reconquista.

In the early days of the Reconquista, several of the kingdoms fought amongst themselves as well as against the Moors. Later, however, they combined forces against the common enemy. By the 1400s, the number of kingdoms had been consolidated to two, Castile and Aragón, which together controlled almost all of the peninsula. By this time, Christian forces had pushed the Moors back to the small kingdom of Granada, on Spain's southern coast. In 1469, Ferdinand, heir to the throne of Aragón, married Isabella, soon to become Queen of Castile. When Ferdinand's father, King John II of Aragón, died in 1479, the two kingdoms were united, completing a process that combined all the independent kingdoms into a single, powerful country. This set the stage for Spain's later role as an imperial power.

The Catholic monarchs, as Ferdinand and Isabella are known, instituted a myriad of social, economic, and legislative reforms in order to strengthen and unify their country. To centralize power under the monarchy, they greatly reduced the power of the aristocracy and took away many of the privileges previously accorded to nobles. At the same time, they sought to capture Granada from the Moors. Victorious Christian forces

Ferdinand and Isabella brought about many changes during their rule, some good and some bad.

finally entered the defeated stronghold in 1492, and Ferdinand and Isabella moved triumphantly into the Alhambra, the former palace of the Moorish kings.

The two sovereigns sought to unify their country in religious faith as well. In 1478, they established the Spanish Inquisition, a court whose stated purpose was to combat heresy by investigating the sincerity of converts to Christianity. Soon, however, the Inquisition broadened its scope and began to persecute all non-Christians. The Jews of Spain had long enjoyed tolerance of their religion by the Moorish overlords and by the kings of Spain, who had come to depend on them in medical, economic, and financial matters. In 1492, however, Ferdinand and Isabella issued an edict that required all Jews—to convert to Christianity or leave Spain. Some Jews converted, but most were forced to sell their property at a great loss and flee their homeland in exile.

In 1502, a similar law was passed regarding the Muslim population, and as a result almost all Muslims converted to Christianity. However, these converts only furnished new targets for the Inquisition: As former "heretics," they were immediately under suspicion. The Spanish Inquisition would continue on its murderous course, employing such inhuman methods for extracting "confessions" as imprisonment, torture, and execution, for more than three centuries. Finally outlawed in 1834, it left a bloody legacy; in their determined quest for unification, the Catholic monarchs robbed their country of much of its native culture, knowledge, and scholarship.

Exploration

As they continued their drive toward unification, Ferdinand and Isabella also sought to increase Spain's power on the world stage. In 1491, an Italian sea captain named Christopher Columbus came to Spain seeking sponsorship for a voyage across the Atlantic Ocean—then called the "Ocean Sea." Columbus believed he could find a profitable new trade route to the Far East—China, Japan, and India. Dreaming of the riches he might find there, Ferdinand and Isabella decided to finance Columbus's expedition. In 1492, with his flagship, *Santa María*, and two smaller ships, the *Niña* and the *Pinta*, Columbus sailed westward across the Atlantic.

For three weeks, the three sailing vessels were pushed along by fair trade winds. But when the voyage grew longer than any previous expedition, the crew threatened to mutiny. Columbus pleaded with them to continue, and they agreed to sail onward for only three more days. At two o'clock on the morning of the second day, a seaman aloft spied a small island—not near China, as Columbus had expected, but in the Bahamas Islands, off the coast of what is now Florida. Columbus had discovered a new continent.

Columbus set about exploring what would later be the Dominican Republic, Haiti, and Cuba before sailing home. The return voyage was actually a greater test of his seamanship than was the voyage west. He had to tack into winds that were blowing against him and endure severe storms before arriving in Spain with the *Niña* and the *Pinta* (the *Santa María* had been wrecked on a reef in Haiti). The king and queen gave him a hero's welcome and bestowed on him the title "Admiral of the Ocean Sea."

On three later voyages, in 1493, 1498, and 1502, Columbus discovered many islands of the Caribbean, including Jamaica and Trinidad. He correctly identified South America as a continent and explored the Central American coastline. In 1494, Spain and Portugal—which was also aggressively exploring the New World—signed the Treaty of Tordesillas, which divided New World territory between the two countries. The next half-century would prove bountiful for Spain. Spanish explorers, soldiers, priests, and adventurers—often drawn from the ranks of the Spanish knights—followed in Columbus's wake, claiming lands for the Spanish crown and establishing the country as a world power.

Cortés and the Aztecs

In 1520, the Spanish adventurer Hernán Cortés led an attack on the Aztec empire, one of the most advanced civilizations of ancient America, located in what is now central and southern Mexico. Tenochtitlán, the Aztec capi-

Cortés conquered the Aztec Empire, putting Mexico under Spain's domination for centuries.

tal, was built upon the islands of shallow Lake Texcoco and had canals, streets of hard earth, and aqueducts to carry fresh water to the city from springs in the nearby hills. At the time of the Spanish invasion, the Aztec empire had a population of between 10 and 12 million, and Tenochtitlán had a population of 100,000.

Montezuma II, the Aztec emperor, had had a premonition that a god named Quetzalcoatl would dethrone him. When Cortés and his armed men marched overland from the eastern coast of Central America and appeared at the capital, Montezuma, convinced that Cortés was Quetzalcoatl, allowed the invaders to occupy his capital city. However, when one of the Spanish officers foolishly allowed his men to slaughter many of the Aztec nobles, the Aztec warriors immediately rose up and drove the Spaniards out of the city. Montezuma was killed in the conflict.

Cortés was a confident commander, and he came up with an ingenious plan. He had his carpenters construct a small fleet of ships, which they then carried in sections to Lake Texcoco, joined together, and set afloat. Directing these 12 warships, Cortés destroyed an attacking fleet of Aztec canoes and marched into the island city over a rebuilt bridge. In bloody fighting—and aided by an epidemic of smallpox that swept through the Aztec population, bringing death to many and weakening their forces—Cortés subdued the Aztec warriors and captured Montezuma's successor, Cuauhtemoc.

Cortés's conquest of the Aztec empire ranks among history's greatest military exploits. The attack spelled the end of the Aztec civilization, which declined rapidly due to disease and disorganization, and opened the way for further conquests in the Americas. Cortés went on to spread Spanish rule to other cities and towns and to be appointed governor of all of New Spain, as Mexico was then known.

Magellan Finds a Way West

While Cortés was battling the Aztecs in Mexico, another courageous explorer was about to bring glory to Spain. In 1519, Ferdinand Magellan,

In a voyage of exploration sponsored by Spain, Portuguese explorer Ferdinand Magellan discovered a passage near the tip of South America that led to the Pacific Ocean.

a Portuguese soldier and adventurer who had served in different parts of the world, led an expedition to find a way around the tip of South America and bring back valuable spices from the East Indies, which he believed lay just beyond the Americas.

Magellan left Spain with a fleet of five ships in September 1519. He sailed into bay after bay along the east coast of South America; finally, in August 1520, he found a stormy and treacherous passage near the tip of South America. In 38 days of difficult and masterful sailing, Magellan brought his ships, now reduced to three, through the wave tossed strait and into the calm of the Pacific Ocean. This passage was later named the Strait of Magellan.

Although his crews considered the expedition at an end and petitioned him to head for home, Magellan pushed on across the Pacific. For 98 long and mutinous days the crew sailed westward. Food and water ran low. Disease broke out aboard ship. The sailors got so hungry they ate sawdust, and men died of starvation. Just in time, they arrived at Guam in the Mariana Islands and found food and water.

Continuing westward, the bold explorer reached the island of Cebu in the Philippine Islands. After converting the local chief to Christianity, Magellan agreed to help him fight a battle with a neighboring island. In the attack, Magellan was killed in a sword fight. However, his dream didn't die: The expedition pressed on, led by Sebastian del Cano and reduced to a single ship. Del Cano found the East Indies and loaded a cargo of cloves, one of the spices Magellan had dreamed of finding. He then sailed around the Cape of Good Hope, at the southern tip of Africa, and headed homeward. On September 8, 1522, Del Cano arrived at Seville, almost three years after the expedition had left those same shores, with only 35 of the original crew of 280. The sale of the cargo of cloves paid for the entire cost of the expedition.

The *Vittoria*, the sole ship that returned from this epic voyage, was the first vessel in history to circumnavigate the globe. The voyage proved beyond a doubt that the earth was truly a sphere.

Pizarro and the Incas

Francisco Pizarro had accompanied the explorer Vasco Núñez de Balboa on a 1513 trip across the narrow Isthmus of Panama, which separates Central and South America. The first European to see the eastern shore of the Pacific, Balboa is said to have waded out into the waves in full armor, held aloft the banner of Castile, and claimed the newly discovered ocean for his country.

In 1531, Pizarro led an expedition of his own to South America in search of the Inca civilization, whose population of six million inhabited an area that stretched 200 miles wide and 2,500 miles in what is now Peru and Bolivia. Aggressive in warfare, the Incas had conquered other peoples and held their empire together by means of a powerful ruler, a strong army, a highly trained bureaucracy, and a sophisticated system of roads that linked the far reaches of the empire. The Incas were rumored to possess great riches, and the promise of such treasure drew Pizarro to the isolated land.

In January 1531, Pizarro set sail for South America with 3 ships, 180 men, 27 horses, and 2 cannon; his partner, Diego de Almagro, later joined him with 130 soldiers and additional horses. Displaying great daring, Pizarro led his band directly into the heart of the Inca empire, high amid the Andes Mountains. Pizarro's men attacked the Incas, slaughtering more than 2,000 in a half-hour massacre and strangling the Inca chieftain, Atahualpa. Atahualpa was the last of the ruling Incas; the empire died with him, broken by the invaders from Europe.

Explorers continued to win prizes for Spain. In 1540, Hernando de Soto, who had accompanied Pizarro and become wealthy as a result of the expedition, led a trek through what is now the southeastern United States. De Soto discovered the Mississippi River and explored territory that would later form nine states. In the 1540s, Francisco Vásquez de Coronado explored parts of the southwestern United States. Although he failed to find the gold he was looking for, his men discovered the magnificent Grand Canyon and the Colorado River.

The Treasure Fleets

For the next century and a half, Spain colonized its new territory and exploited the resources its explorers had discovered. Each spring, a fleet of ships sailed from Spain to the Caribbean carrying supplies, including wine, cloth, ironwork, books, and, most important, mercury to be used in the process of extracting silver from the ore mines of Peru. After the ships unloaded their European goods, they filled their holds with fabulous cargos of gold, silver, jewels, and agricultural products that would enrich Spanish merchants and permit Spanish kings to fight their seemingly endless wars with England, the Netherlands, and France. They also loaded vegetables and wines for the return voyage, gunpowder for each ship's arsenal of guns, royal revenues from court fines, and money from the sale of papal indulgences, purchased from the church as penances for the commission of sins.

In recent years, treasure-hunting divers have discovered the remains of one of these vessels, the armed galleon *Atocha*, which sank off the tip of Florida during a storm in 1622. From their dives to the wreck and from the ship's manifest, found in an archive in Spain, the divers learned that this particular galleon was armed with 20 bronze cannon, 60 muskets, and ample powder and shot for 82 soldiers. There were 18 gunners and 115 other crewmen and boys.

Crowded into small cabins in the ship's high sterncastle were 48 passengers, including high-ranking Catholic priests, a Spanish leader of Cuzco, Peru, and wealthy Peruvian merchants. New World wealth was stored in the ship's holds and storerooms. Together with copper, indigo, and tobacco, the *Atocha* carried an immense treasure—901 silver bars, 161 gold bars or discs, and about 255,000 silver coins. The cargo also included 20,000 pesos for the heirs of Christopher Columbus, sizable sums from papal indulgences, and money from a head tax on black slaves.

By 1550, as a result of its New World conquests, Spain controlled Mexico, Central America, much of western South America, part of what is now the southwestern United States, nearly all of the islands of the Caribbean—known as the West Indies—and the Philippine Islands, then called the East Indies. Spanish traders dominated the colonies' early economic life, and both the conquered peoples and the new settlers were subject to the laws of distant Spanish kings, with little voice in their own affairs. Missionaries arrived to convert the conquered native peoples, whom they considered "heathens" because they did not believe in the God of the Bible, to Christianity. The missionaries also built schools and churches and taught the Indians to speak Spanish, which became the official language of most of Central and South America (with the major exception of Brazil, where Portuguese is spoken). Today, 9 out of 10 people in Latin America (Mexico, Central America, and South America) speak Spanish.

Between 1791 and 1824 most New World colonies fought wars of independence and freed themselves from European rule. Since then, Spain has exercised little influence over the political life of her former colonies; however, Latin Americans still look to Spain as the source of much of their culture as well as their language and religion.

Philip II built up a powerful Spanish fleet that he thought was invincible.

From World Power to Outcast

In the days when absolute monarchs ruled in Spain and other countries of Europe, royal family alliances often determined who would become king or queen. So it was in Spain. In 1496, Isabella and Ferdinand's daughter Juana married Prince Philip of the Habsburg dynasty of Germany and Austria. When Juana—known as "La Loca" (the crazy one)—was judged incompetent to reign, her husband became Philip I of Spain. In 1516, their 17-year-old son became Charles I of Spain, and in 1519 the new king was crowned Charles V of the Habsburg or Holy Roman Empire. The unified Spanish and Habsburg dynasties became one of the largest empires in history and ruled most of central and southern Europe between France and Poland. It was at this time that Spain seized the Canary Islands and the Balearic Islands.

Charles's dream of a Catholic empire led him into wars with other European countries, where Protestant opposition had risen up against Catholic regimes. (This 16th-century period in Europe is called the Reformation.) In the New World, Charles encouraged the adventuresome *conquistadores* to conquer more lands for Spain, and within a few years Spain governed a vast territory in Europe and the Americas that was many times its own size. Spain, it was said, was "mistress of the world and queen of the ocean."

In 1588, the English inflicted a disastrous defeat on the Spanish Armada, which led

But Spain enjoyed only a brief period of world glory. The vast income from its New World colonies was not translated into prosperity at home. Instead, this wealth was spent to fight recurring wars, quell internal revolts, carry on the Inquisition, and support the large Catholic priesthood. Charles's son Philip II, a rigid and determined sovereign who reigned from 1556 to 1598, established a new capital at Madrid and then embarked on a series of disastrous wars. Perhaps Philip's biggest mistake was to try to win England back to the Catholic faith. In 1588, he sent the famed Spanish Armada to land on British soil—but wound up losing more than half

eventually to Spain's demise as a world-class power.

the Armada's 130 warships and two-thirds of its men in a battle with the British fleet in the English channel off the coast of France. The conflict cost Spain its supremacy at sea and much political prestige.

Although the 16th and 17th centuries saw a flowering of cultural and intellectual life in Spain, Spanish power declined steadily in the 1600s because of inept and inefficient administration of both the home country and its overseas empire. The Spanish monarchs failed to adapt to changing times, and the country fell behind the rest of Europe in industrial development, constitutional government, intellectual freedom, and education. Poor working conditions at home and the lure of glistening gold in the Americas drew young men to the colonies, further draining the country of its native talent. The author Cervantes caught the mood of the era when he wrote of "the poverty of some, the greed of others, and the madness of all."

In 1700, Charles II, the last of the Habsburg kings, died, leaving no heirs. Because of intermarriage among the royalty of Europe, several pretenders (those with a claim) sought the Spanish throne. The ultimate ascension of Philip of Anjou, grandson of King Louis XIV of the Bourbon dynasty in France and great-grandson of Spain's Philip III, unleashed the War of the Spanish Succession, in which France and Spain opposed England, the Netherlands, and the Holy Roman Empire. Although the newly crowned Philip V maintained his throne, Spain lost parts of its empire, including Gibraltar, which it ceded to Great Britain, giving the British access to the Mediterranean.

A series of Bourbon kings attempted to moderate Spain's foreign policy and bring the economy under control. Bourbon rule was interrupted in 1808, when French troops under Emperor Napoleon I invaded Spain and placed Napoleon's brother Joseph on the throne. This French intrusion was short-lived: In 1813, a combined force from Britain, Portugal, and Spain forced the French out in the Peninsular War, and Spain restored its Bourbon monarchy. More Bourbon sovereigns followed.

In 1873, internal strife led to the establishment of a republican government (one which is managed by elected representatives). However, after a year's time, domestic problems were no better. When it became apparent that the First Republic had failed, the Bourbon dynasty was restored.

Throughout this period, Spain continued to have trouble managing its colonies. In 1898, during Spanish attempts to suppress a growing independence movement in Cuba and the Philippines, a mysterious explosion sank the U.S. battleship *Maine*, which had been sent to Havana to protect American citizens there. Two hundred and sixty sailors were killed in the

In 1898, the U.S. battleship Maine *was blown up in the harbor of Havana, leading to the Spanish-American War.*

explosion, and the United States declared war on Spain. As a result of the Spanish-American War, Spain ceded Puerto Rico, the Philippine Islands, and Guam to the United States and granted Cuba its independence. These were among the last of Spain's colonial possessions. A once-mighty empire had crumbled.

By the beginning of the 20th century, the Spanish monarchy seemed out of step with the rest of the country. Unrestrained kings had long exercised nearly absolute authority, granting special privileges to a few members of the nobility and an inordinate amount of power to the Catholic church. The tides of religious reformation and republican government that had brought changes to other countries of Europe finally caught up with Spain in the 1930s. In a 1931 election, citizens voted overwhelmingly for a republican form of government. King Alphonso XIII was forced to leave the country, and Spain's Cortes (parliament) adopted a new democratic constitution.

Among its far-reaching provisions, the Second Republic's constitution guaranteed equality before the law, renounced war as an instrument of national policy, separated the Catholic church from the government (thus destroying much of the church's power and influence), removed privileges from the religious orders, stated that there should be no official religion, abolished titles for the nobility, extended the right to vote to all male and female citizens over the age of 23, and provided for free and compulsory primary education in government instead of church schools.

As the young republic moved to implement these drastic changes in the social and economic fabric of the country, it met with intense opposi-

The Spanish Civil War raged for 32 months and ended with the establishment of a dictatorship under Francisco Franco.

tion from large landowners and the church. This period also coincided with a worldwide depression, and Spain was not spared the dire economic consequences: Exports fell, labor strikes broke out, poverty became widespread, and violence increased as peasants seized land from the *latifundia*, or large estates of the wealthy landowners. Catholic church buildings were destroyed and priests were attacked. Conflicts between political factions led to increasing violence, and political murders became commonplace. Clearly, revolt was in the air.

Civil War

On July 17, 1936, Spanish army general Francisco Franco led a rebellion of nationalist anti-leftist forces stationed in Morocco. Backed by large landowners, the church, and those who favored a return to the monarchy, Franco captured several towns in the south of Spain, attempting to recap-

ture the capital, Madrid, and quickly moved northward. Government forces, called Loyalists, fought and held Franco back, and the conflict grew into a long and bloody civil war.

The Communist regime in the Soviet Union provided help to the Loyalists, sending weapons, ammunition, and advisors. Although the western powers agreed to remain neutral, Loyalist sympathizers from the United States and Europe organized an "International Brigade" to fight the Nationalists. Franco found support from Fascist Italy and Nazi Germany. Nationalist forces quickly eclipsed the strength of the Loyalists.

The Spanish Civil War drew international attention. A number of noted journalists and authors went to Spain to report on the war. Ernest Hemingway's 1940 novel *For Whom The Bell Tolls* draws on his wartime experiences in Spain, and George Orwell wrote of his disillusionment with the Loyalist cause in his 1938 *Homage to Catalonia*. In the aftermath of the Nationalist bombing of a Basque village, the world-renowned Spanish artist Pablo Picasso painted an enormous work he named "Guernica," after that village.

On April 1, 1939, after 32 months of heavy fighting, Franco emerged victorious. By the end of the war, more than one million Spaniards had died on the battlefield or in hospitals. Franco later constructed a mammoth cross and basilica in memory of the many Spaniards who died in the civil war; called "El Valle de los Caidos" (The Valley of the Fallen), it is located near Madrid.

Franco named himself *caudillo*, leader of the nation. He established a dictatorial regime in which he was chief of state, commander-in-chief of the armed forces, and head of the only political party that was allowed. In addition, he oversaw the adoption of a set of "Fundamental Laws" to replace the former republican constitution. Franco treated the defeated Loyalists harshly, putting two million people into prison or penal battalions. Others he ordered executed.

Postwar Spain was economically devastated. Many farmers had lost their agricultural machinery and their houses, and some 200 towns had

(continued on page 65)

SCENES OF
SPAIN

➤ *The Plaza Mayor in Madrid evokes the glory of Spain's past history.*

◄ *The* corrida, *bullfighting, is almost a national symbol of Spain.*

At the southernmost tip of Spain lies the strategically important Rock of Gibraltar, which has been controlled for almost two centuries by Britain.

◄
The imposing Alcazar in Segovia was formerly the palace of Queen Isabella.

Y *Andalusia, a southern province, has palm trees and other tropical foliage.*

➤ *Country life has been little affected by the vast changes in the urban centers of Spain.*

∀ *Flamenco music and dance is a unique expression of the Spanish soul.*

⋏ *Sheep are Spain's chief livestock product.*

◄ *Madrid, the capital, is Spain's most modern, international, and cosmopolitan city.*

➤
Olives are one of Spain's major agricultural exports.

▲ *Many structures in Spain, such as this bridge in Merida, were built by the Romans.*

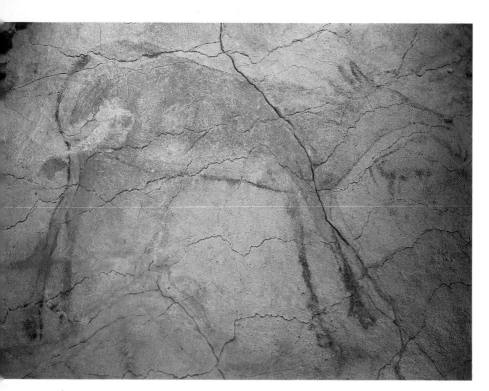

Λ *The prehistoric cave
paintings at Altamira are
amazingly well preserved.*

➤ *The Spanish painter Goya
was a sardonic
commentator on his times,
as in this portrait of Carlos
IV from the Prado.*

been so badly damaged that the Franco government had to step in and rebuild them. One-third of all railway locomotives and cars had been destroyed. There was little money left in the treasury. To make matters worse, World War II began only a few months after the Spanish Civil War ended. Although officially neutral, Franco supported Hitler's Nazi Germany and Mussolini's Italy and sent Spanish soldiers to fight alongside German troops. He also shipped raw materials to Germany. At the war's end, because of Franco's wartime aid to Germany and Italy, Spain was excluded from the United Nations, a peacekeeping organization set up by the victorious Allies. (Spain was finally invited to join the organization in 1955.)

After World War II, Spain showed some economic and political liberalization. Labor strikes were held illegally in the 1950s and increased during the 1960s; in 1965, workers were finally granted the right to strike. There was gradual tolerance of long-suppressed political opposition, and in 1966 the strict press censorship that Franco had imposed after taking power was relaxed. An issue of growing concern was the separatist demands of the far northern regions of Catalonia and the Basque country. These regions, which are ethnically and culturally different from neighboring regions, had persistently sought autonomy during the 20th century. Although the Catalan movement was moderate, revolutionary Basque nationalists formed a terrorist organization called ETA and began asserting their demands with violence.

During the 1960s, as the conservative Franco regime relaxed its harsh social and economic controls, Spain reestablished contact with the rest of western Europe. However, most western governments remained hostile to Spain as long as Franco was in power. When Franco died in 1975, Spain's political and economic climate changed dramatically. First, following a plan that Franco had prepared, the monarchy was restored. Prince Juan Carlos de Borbon, grandson of the last Spanish king, Alphonso XIII, became head of state as King Juan Carlos I. Spain then adopted a democratic political system, led by a parliament (the Cortes) and a prime minister, in

José María Aznar, head of the Popular party, appeared in public soon after an assassination attempt involving a car bomb planted by Basque separatists in April 1995. The next year, he became prime minister as a result of national elections.

which the king serves only as a figurehead with powers limited to advisory and ceremonial duties.

In 1978, under Prime Minister Adolfo Suárez González, the Spanish Cortes adopted a new democratic constitution. The constitution recognized for the first time a number of political parties, paving the way for the 1982 victory of Spain's Socialist party in national elections. Felipe González, head of the Socialist party, was elected prime minister. The Socialists won the next three general elections as well, ruling Spain until 1996, when José María Aznar of the conservative Popular party took over as the head of a coalition government.

By 1982, with Franco gone and democracy in place, Spain was accepted into the diplomatic ranks of western Europe. The country joined NATO in 1982. Then in 1986, after years of planning, Spain became a member of the European Economic Community, which later evolved into the European Union (EU). By joining this organization, Spain's leaders began the process of integrating their country's economy with those of other European nations, opening up new markets for Spanish products.

Spain manufactures more automobiles than any other nation in Europe, but most of these cars are produced for and sold by companies in other countries.

The Economy

About 15.5 million people work for a living in Spain, out of a total population of 39 million; 60 percent of these workers are male and 40 percent are female. Some 60 percent of all working Spaniards earn their living by providing services to others, particularly in the country's growing tourism industry. About 30 percent work in industry and construction, 10 percent in agriculture and fishing.

Spain's basic unit of currency is the *peseta*; in 1996, $1 U.S. was equal to approximately 127 pesetas. In 1995, Spain's gross national product (the total value of all goods and services a country produces in one year) was $565 billion U.S. The country's per capita income was $14,300 U.S.

Agriculture

Almost all of Spain's tillable land is used for farming, either as cropland or pastureland. Agricultural production remains low, however, because of poor soil, the dry climate, and inefficient farming methods. The government has introduced irrigation to help farmers increase their crop yield and open up uncultivated lands. Irrigation has increased food production by one-third, yet Spain still lags behind other European nations.

About two-thirds of Spain's farmers own their own land; the remainder work as hired employees or tenants (those who live and work on somebody else's farm). A few hereditary owners possess large tracts of land, a legacy of earlier times when a monarch granted huge landholdings to his nobles. Even now, 50 percent of the farmland is owned by only one percent of the people. Large estates, or *latifundia*, predominate in the south. Small farmers own most of the land in the north, but many of these farms consist of only a few acres.

Crops of wheat and other cereal grains grow in the north and on the central plain; these crops account for more than 60 percent of Spain's cultivated land. Farmers in the south and east produce the country's grapes, olives, oranges, and other citrus fruits. Olive trees and vineyards are spread over large areas; Spain is the world's largest producer of olives and olive oil and the fourth-largest producer of wine. The country is also a leading producer of cork.

Sheep are Spain's chief livestock product. Also raised for profit are beef cattle, chickens, goats, and pigs. Fishing has traditionally been a

About two-thirds of Spain's farmers own their own land; the remainder work as hired hands or tenants.

major occupation, and fish is an important part of the Spanish diet. However, in recent years the fishing industry has declined in importance as the coastal waters, once rich with fish and shellfish, have been largely depleted. The best remaining fishing grounds are in the Bay of Biscay, off the country's northern coast, where Spanish boats haul their catches of anchovies, codfish, whiting, and hake. The country is experimenting with breeding fish in ponds on the shore and then releasing the young fish into the ocean to replace the ones being caught, a process that would help meet the strong demand from Spain's many fish markets.

Manufacturing and Mining

Most of Spain's industrial plants are clustered around the cities of Madrid, Bilbao, and Barcelona. Spain's major metal industries are iron and steel, which are produced in the north and constitute the country's most important export. Other major products are ships, chemicals, rubber, machinery, and electronics. The country is an important producer of consumer goods such as autos, refrigerators, and televisions; textiles; shoes and leather goods; toys; and furniture. The automobile industry is Spain's biggest employer and also a major export; Spain is the top auto exporting country in Europe, although most of the cars are produced and sold under the names of companies from other nations. These companies operate dozens of large manufacturing plants in Spain.

Most minerals are found in the Cantabrian Mountains of northern Spain. The country's most valuable mineral is mercury, but there are also significant deposits of potash, uranium, copper, lead, zinc, and coal. Major natural gas fields were discovered in the 1970s in the Pyrenees, and small fields of oil have been located offshore in the Atlantic Ocean and Mediterranean Sea; however, Spain must import most of the oil it needs for domestic consumption.

By 1980, the value of Spain's industrial production had reached two and a half times that of its agricultural production. But rapid industrialization has brought problems as well. Many factories remain small, employing fewer than 30 workers. This is particularly true in the food-processing industry, where much of the equipment is old-fashioned. Industry suffers from a lack of skilled workers and a need for better technical training.

Power

Spain relies increasingly on imported oil and nuclear energy to generate the electricity it needs to run its new industries and provide power for home use. Hydroelectric power plants provide two-fifths of the country's needs, but all the rivers with enough water flow for hydroelectric power have already been dammed. Spain's first nuclear power plant opened in 1969; by 1995, nuclear power supplied 14 percent of the country's energy requirement. The existence of extensive deposits of uranium, which is used to fuel nuclear reactors, makes the development of more nuclear power plants a possibility.

Tourism

While the number of people working in Spain's traditional field of agriculture is decreasing, the number employed in tourism continues to grow. The tourist industry in Spain grew from 6 million visitors in 1960 to 39 million in 1995, making the country the third-largest tourist center in Europe (behind only France and Italy). Within the service sector of the economy, the tourist industry now employs one of every 10 Spanish workers. Foreigners are attracted by Spain's colorful festivals, picturesque castles, and traditional bullfights—and by consumer prices that are lower than those in most European countries and the United States. With its balmy climate, the south of Spain has become the "sunbelt" of Europe.

Most tourists come from France, Portugal, Germany, Great Britain, and the United States. Approximately one-third of all northern Europeans who vacation along the Mediterranean go to Spain. The Balearic Islands, off Spain's southern coast, offer the greatest number of tourist accommodations in Spain, followed by the Costa Brava in Catalonia, the Costa del Sol in Andalusia, and the Canary Islands.

Despite its upsurge in tourism, Spain remains behind most other European countries in its standard of living. The Spanish worker earns substantially less than other West Europeans, and the country's unemployment rate remains high. In recent years, many workers have had to go to neighboring countries to find jobs; a number of these workers lack the skills necessary to work in a modern industrial plant or in specialized agriculture. However, Spain's growing entrepreneurial class, its astonishingly high rate of literacy (97 percent), and the continued expansion of its tourist industry, among other positive factors, could bring better times and a stronger economic future.

Most Basques wear the traditional felt cap, which is much like the beret worn in France, on the other side of the Pyrenees Mountains.

Regions, Cities, and Culture

In Spain, people who live in different regions have distinctive cultures and traditions. The country's history of invasion and settlement by people from various backgrounds has created a cultural collage. Through time, these vastly different cultures and ethnic groups have developed in their own ways, influenced by climate, geography, racial inheritance, and other factors.

During the era of the Christian kings, some of the independent kingdoms acted like separate countries. Their inhabitants developed their own customs and manner of dress—even their own languages. The kingdoms were able to preserve their individual traditions even after Spain became united under a monarchy and later under the Franco dictatorship. In Spain today, if you ask a Spanish man where he is from, he will most likely answer, "I am a son of Castile," or "I am a son of Andalusia," reflecting this deep loyalty to native region.

For example, the difference in speech between a native of Catalonia and a native of the Basque region of the north is as great as the difference between a Spaniard and a Portuguese. In many areas, children speak only their local dialect until they enter school. There they learn "Castilian" Spanish, the official language of the country that is spoken by three-fourths of the population.

Spain's 1978 constitution recognized these regional differences. Taking into account each region's "common historic, cultural, and economic characteristics," the constitution allowed the regions to group together into 17 autonomous communities, with the power to govern themselves as long as their laws did not conflict with the interests of Spain as a whole. By 1983, all 17 communities had finalized their autonomous statutes and become the autonomous communities of Andalusia, Aragón, Asturias, Balearic Islands, Canary Islands, Cantabria, Castile-La Mancha, Castile-León, Catalonia, Valencia, Extremadura, Galicia, Madrid, Murcia, Navarre, Basque Country, and Rioja.

Catalonia

This region, located in the northeastern part of the country, has long been associated with southern France and its people. The six million people

Each region of Spain has its distinctive native garb. These men are dressed in the traditional costumes of Navarre.

who occupy Catalonia and the nearby Balearic Islands speak Catalan, a language related to the Provençal tongue of southern France and quite different from Castilian Spanish.

Under Franco, the teaching of Catalan in the schools was forbidden. The people interpreted this as a slur on their heritage. The 1978 constitution restored their right to their own language; now street signs in Barcelona, the region's major city, are printed in both Catalan and Castilian, schooling is in Catalan, and there is a Catalan newspaper and radio station.

New industries are springing up in the region, and foreign companies from as far away as Japan are building plants in Barcelona, adding to its cosmopolitan character. In the cafés along its tree-lined boulevards and in its shops, the salespersons speak Catalan (although they will often switch to Castilian if that will help clinch a sale). The language does present an occasional problem to workers who come to Catalonia from elsewhere in Spain.

Basque Country

The oldest identifiable ethnic group in western Europe, the Basques are believed to be descendants of the original Iberians who inhabited the peninsula 5,000 years ago. Their language, Euskara, is unlike any other tongue in the world and is probably derived from the languages of these ancient inhabitants. Three million Basques live in the far north of Spain and across the border in France; they have an ancient disdain for political borders such as these.

Basques are different from other Spaniards in physical appearance as well as in language and customs. Basque people tend to be short, wide of shoulder and hips, and to have short, sturdy legs. Anthropologists have discovered evidence of racial differences through blood tests: Basques have a lower incidence of Type B blood and a higher incidence of Type O blood than do other Europeans. They also have a higher incidence of Rh negative blood type.

Throughout history the Basques have earned their living from the sea and the land. In earlier times they were expert fishermen, sailing the North Atlantic in search of whales. Basques led voyages of exploration in the New World in the 1500s and later turned to piracy and smuggling. Today, many have taken jobs in the shipyards, steel mills, and metalworking plants of the industrialized city of Bilbao—where Spain's largest blast furnaces were built to take advantage of the nearby iron ore and plentiful coal supply.

Some Basques continue to work their farms, growing wheat, corn, beans, rye, grapes, and alfalfa. Others raise livestock and sheep in mountain pastures. Family plots of land are closely held and are passed along to succeeding generations. Because the family plots are so small, modern farm machinery is scarce in this region.

Basques take great pride in their cooking, as shown by the hundred or more "eating clubs" scattered about the region. Members of these all-male clubs gather weekly to prepare and serve a meal to fellow club members. Basque seafood dishes are legendary and have earned a worldwide reputation.

The Basques have long been a people apart. Until modern times it was almost unheard of for a Basque man or woman to marry outside the clan, and for centuries the Basques have fiercely resisted being absorbed by other peoples. Such independence of spirit has also ignited small terrorist groups who have committed acts of violence against the Spanish government—including bombings, kidnappings, and assassinations—in an effort to gain their independence from Spain and France.

Galicia

In Galicia, located in Spain's northwestern corner, many inhabitants speak a dialect of Portuguese known as Gallego. Native Galicians are descendents of the Celtic tribes that invaded Spain in the first millennium B.C. The region has a long history of fighting for its independence; it was to this far corner of the country that many Spaniards retreated during medieval times when the rest of Spain fell under Moorish rule. Galician language and traditions, as well as the medieval churches that dot the hillsides, remain from that era.

Galicia's fertile, mountainous terrain produces crops of fruit for export. Because of the region's hereditary land tenure system, individual properties have been subdivided over so many generations that some land-owners own only a small tract of woods, an old mill, or a single tree on a tiny plot. Needless to say, farming on such small plots is unproductive.

Old ways persist in this secluded region. Galicians still believe in ancestor worship and regard the dead as possible tormentors of the living, who must appease them by offering food. The holy city of Santiago de Compostela, one of the three chief European places of pilgrimage during the Middle Ages, is the contemporary religious and cultural heart of the region.

Castile-León, Castile-La Mancha, and Madrid

Historically, Castile has been the geographic, political, psychological, and artistic heartland of Spain. The kingdom of Castile, allied with the king-dom of Aragón, led the struggle to defeat the Moors, and the Castilian is even now regarded as the country's symbol—dignified, enduring, coura-geous. Castilians have also been conditioned by the hard climate and lone-liness of their plateau region; many are proud, some say even arrogant.

By 1983, when Spain's 17 autonomous communities drew up their final borders, the traditional regions of Castile and León became the autonomous communities of Castile-León, Castile-La Mancha, and the one-province community of Madrid (which also contains Spain's capital city of Madrid). In 1561, Philip II decided to place his court in Madrid, then a small town, because it was at the geographic center of the penin-sula; today, the capital city is the center of political life, administration, and banking for the entire country.

The city of Madrid is a magnet for tourists, who come to see its impos-ing historic buildings, its famous museums, and the renowned museum of art called the Prado. Distinctive hotels and restaurants line Madrid's broad boulevards. As one of the major cities of the world, Madrid has the usual rush-hour traffic jams and problems with pollution; however, visitors find it convenient to get around the city on a subway system that has 10 lines and 100 stations. One of the most popular tourist sights is the Royal Palace (King Juan Carlos I actually lives in the Zarzuela Palace outside the city). Madrid's population has doubled since 1960 and now includes more than three million residents. Some 100,000 students, many of them from Latin American countries, attend the University of Madrid.

Other Regions

The remaining regions preserve their own ethnic differences, distinctive traits, customs, and traditions. Many people in the northern autonomous community of Asturias have blond hair, a reminder that centuries ago the Celtic people swept down from northern Europe. In Andalusia, in southern Spain, many have the dark skin and dark eyes of their Moorish ancestors.

Andalusia's Moorish heritage sets the tone for this autonomous community. Seville, the country's fourth-largest city, is its capital. Seville's cathedral, built in the 15th century to celebrate the expulsion of the Moors, is the third-largest cathedral in the world after St. Peter's in Rome and St. Paul's in London. In Toledo are found magnificent edifices that reflect not only Moorish but Christian and Jewish devotion. The Cathedral of Toledo took two centuries to build and has a stately tower 295 feet (90 meters) high, one of the most impressive in all Europe. The entire city—with its winding, cobblestoned streets and architectural treasures—has been designated a national monument.

Gypsies

One ethnic group exists that has no geographic community. As in other countries of Europe, Gypsies wander from place to place and are a deprived minority. They can be seen on the roads and streets, driving

Spain has a sizeable Gypsy population. Flamenco music and dance is one of their contributions to Spanish culture.

carts, begging, and peddling. There are several hundred thousand Gypsies in Spain. The largest Gypsy communities are found in Granada, Madrid, Barcelona, and Murcia.

Many of these wandering folk can no longer find seasonal work in farming. As a result, a number of Gypsies have moved to cities and become part of the Spanish work force. They hold regular jobs, send their children to school, and have given up the nomadic life.

Country Life

Although Spain's recent industrialization has brought vast changes to the country's cosmopolitan centers, country life has been little affected. Most rural towns are set up following a traditional pattern, presided over by a castle and a church. In the center of the town is the *plaza mayor,* the town's principal square, which is surrounded on all sides by shops and homes, with the church at one side. In the evening, the plaza is the scene of the daily *paseo,* when people stroll along the sidewalks and chat. Older people sit on benches or at tables in sidewalk cafes to watch the passing parade.

A typical rural home is made of stone and clay. Its exterior is white-washed to reflect the heat of the sun and keep the interior cool. Houses usually have a gently sloping tile roof and decorative iron grillwork at the windows and are built close to the street.

Most of Spain's farmers live in these villages and small towns. Each morning and evening they travel over dirt roads to and from their fields at the edge of town, either walking or riding in a donkey cart. Since electricity has reached most of the villages, farmers are increasingly making use of farm machinery. Not many years ago most farmers had only donkey power to help them plow, plant, and harvest their crops; today, many of them have been able to purchase tractors. Better fertilizers have also become available, which enable the farmers to grow more abundant crops. However, country life has changed less in the last 30 years than city life, and agriculture has fallen behind industry in overall economic importance to the country. The standard of living in rural areas is lower than that in the cities; as a result, hundreds of thousands of farmers have taken jobs in factories or are among those who have gone to other countries to find work.

In dress, many farmers in the outlying areas wear a black hat called a *boina*. Men wear this hat both for work and for dress. Rural women commonly wear full skirts and a blouse or plain dress.

City Life

Marked changes have taken place in Spain's cities since the 1950s. As employment opportunities increased—accompanied by a rise in the level of living for wage earners—modern, urban ways of life were quickly adopted. Most city dwellers now live in apartments, and almost all city housing now has electricity.

As in earlier times, workers spend much of their earnings on food, clothing, and other necessities for their families. However, Spain's recent economic expansion has enabled more Spaniards than ever to buy television sets, refrigerators, cars, even computers. Many young people work at odd jobs to earn money that they spend on clothes, cassettes, CDs, and motor scooters and at discotheques.

The industrialization of the country has blurred the old differences between Spain's rich and poor. For centuries, Spanish society was divided into social classes, with little opportunity for a person to move from a lower class to a higher one. Now, while the old wealthy aristocratic class maintains its traditions and inherited lands, a new middle class provides a demand for consumer goods and for the latest foreign fashions.

In the past 50 years, the lifestyles of young men and women have greatly changed. For women the change has been dramatic. Two generations ago it was unthinkable for an upper- or middle-class woman to work. In 1940, only 14 percent of Spanish women worked. By 1995, 35 percent of women were participating in the labor force. Women who used to work as maids have moved up the employment ladder to take jobs in restaurants and stores. Others study to become doctors, lawyers, journalists, or musicians or to work in government or business.

The way people buy their food and clothing has changed as well. In the old days, the family's needs were taken care of by small neighborhood shops. Housewives went from the fish store to the butcher to the greengrocer. Everything was fresh and was cooked and eaten on the day it was purchased. Although such shops still exist, more and more people go to the large city markets that sell everything from wine to soap. Clothes and household goods may be found in large department stores, and there are many specialty stores and boutiques. Leather shops feature wallets, handbags, and cases in the classic Spanish style. Footwear also draws shopper attention, with *zapaterías* (sandal vendors) lining the streets in large cities and towns. Madrid has one street—Fuencarral—that has shoe stores from one end to the other.

Until recently, traditional shopping hours lasted from 9 A.M. to 1:30 or 2 P.M., and 4:30 to 8 P.M. The long midday pause gives shopkeepers the chance to have their own leisurely lunch before returning to the store, where they work until early evening. Recently, these shops have been replaced by larger supermarkets, which remain open all day long. Most factories and offices also close for a three-hour midday break and then reopen until 7 P.M. Some Spaniards still take the traditional *siesta* (rest period) after lunch, although most people no longer follow this custom.

In the evenings, families will often go out for a paseo before the evening meal, which they do not eat until 10 or 11 P.M. They may stop into a *tasca*, a small tavern that specializes in *tapas*, bite-size snacks made of a variety of foods such as squid, mussels, pieces of fish, tortilla, snails, shrimp, or *jamon Serrano* (thinly sliced ham), or they may stop at a sidewalk café to visit with friends and drink coffee, soft drinks, or wine. Many young professionals also stop in their favorite café for an *aperitivo* in the late afternoon before heading home from work. Most cafés in the cities are crowded from 7 to 9 P.M., as groups of friends meet to converse with one another and to trade ideas. In earlier times, cafés were the meeting places for groups of famous writers and artists, who would hold a *tertulia*—or café gathering—at a particular café on a particular day.

Food

Most Spanish food is not highly seasoned and is served warm, not hot. Vegetables and salads are usually served as a first course. Fish, a popular food in Spain, is available in most cities, even those far from the water. Hake, monkfish, tuna, and swordfish are on many menus, as is *calamares* (squid).

A staple of the Spanish diet is pulses—dried beans, lentils, or chick peas, usually cooked together with pieces of sausage or other meat. Another favorite, originally from Valencia, is *paella*—a rice-based dish flavored with saffron and embellished with many tidbits of seafood, meat, or chicken. In Andalusia a favorite dish is *gazpacho*, a cold vegetable soup that has been described as a "liquid salad." For dessert, oranges, melons, dates, peaches, or grapes are often served along with a piece of cheese.

Sidewalk cafes are an integral part of Spanish social life.

A glass of wine is popular before or during a meal. Until recently, most Spanish wines were used only to blend with better-known foreign wines, particularly those from France. Now winemakers bottle several types of Spanish wine and sell them in the export market. A well-known wine is *rioja*, a red table wine made from grapes grown in the Ebro valley. Sherry is popular in Spain and comes from vineyards at the southern tip of the peninsula. One sherry that is particularly admired by connoisseurs is *amontillado*, which has a flavor that reminds people of hazelnuts.

Fiestas

Fiestas—festivals that are usually held as part of a religious event—play an important part in Spanish life, both rural and urban. People dress up in colorful costumes of their region, join in dancing in the street, show off their local crafts, and enjoy the distinctive food of their locale. Each province has its own unique costume, and often different villages within the same province have their own distinctive modes of dress.

Celebrations are held throughout the calendar year. The *romería* takes place in rural areas and consists of a long cavalcade of horsemen that travels to pay homage to a shrine. The most famous romería is a Gypsy pilgrimage to El Rocío, in the province of Huelva, to a small church where a statue of the Virgin Mary is believed to have miraculous powers. The men on horseback escort white-covered wagons garlanded with flowers, shawls, and paper streamers, while the women ride in the wagons or on horseback behind the men. The cavalcade makes its way through the olive trees of Andalusia to the sound of singing, castanets, guitars, and laughter. After the religious ceremony, which is still held on a Sunday, the Gypsies spend the rest of the day dancing, resting, and watching a bullfight, then head for home the following Monday.

The *verbena* is a night festival that is held on the eve of a religious holiday. Common throughout Spain, this festival is put on in towns or in city neighborhoods and features singing and dancing.

The *falla* is a festival devoted to deflating the egos of the high and mighty. The best-known falla is held in Valencia in March to celebrate St. Joseph's Day. To prepare for the celebration, craftsmen make large effigies—caricatures of famous people, political figures, and city officials—out of cardboard, papier mâché, or wood. Most offices and shops close after lunch on the festival day, and autos are banned from the streets and squares as the cleverly painted figures are paraded through the streets.

On the last night of the celebration, a prize is awarded to the best figure and the rest are set on fire. The townspeople dance all night by the firelight in their colorful costumes. Girls wearing the traditional *mantilla* (lacy shawl or scarf) over a high comb ride on floats decorated with thousands of carnations. Orchestras play, and illuminated balloons float into the sky while fireworks arch overhead. The winning figure is later placed in a museum—the Museo del Minot Indultat (better known as Museo Fallero) in Valencia. The day after the festival, workers start on the next year's figures.

The city of Jeréz, in Andalusia, is noted for its *feria*, or fair, held each year in May. Men wearing tight-fitting jackets, soft leather boots, and wide-brimmed hats ride the fine horses that are raised in the region. Women wearing mantillas and brightly colored skirts ride in open carriages festooned with flowers. There are bullfights, horse races, dancing in the streets, and sampling of local sherry.

Semana Santa (Holy Week) is celebrated by processions of varying magnificence in every town, village, and hamlet in Spain. Holy Week in Seville each year attracts thousands of tourists from all over the world. Granada, too, offers a dramatic—if less famous—spectacle. On Friday night, images of saints and tableaus representing scenes from Jesus's last days are carried through the darkened streets. Hundreds of candles illuminate the gold, jewels, silks, and brocades used to fashion the tableaus. On either side of the procession march the penitents, barefoot, eyes shining through narrow slits in their high, pointed, black-and-white hoods. A single drum beat sets the pace for the procession while the cathedral bell tolls in a lament for the dead.

One of the biggest and noisiest festivals of the year takes place each July in Pamplona in Navarre—10 days of dancing, masquerades, and merrymaking. Called the *Sanfermines*, it has been a tradition since the 1500s. The climax comes when attendants drive six fighting bulls down the cobblestone streets toward the arena where the traditional bullfight will be held. Young men run just ahead of the bulls in the half-mile dash, dodging the dangerous animals and risking bumps, bruises, or a goring to prove their manly courage. The yearly event is so popular it is shown on nationwide television.

Sport

Most Spaniards are enthusiastic sports fans. They are particularly enthusiastic about soccer, which they call *fútbol*. Every Sunday, stadiums all over Spain fill up with 40,000 to 50,000 spectators who come to cheer their favorite soccer teams. In Madrid, up to 135,000 people crowd into the main stadium to see the famous Real Madrid team, which qualifies as one of the best in Europe. In Spain, leading soccer players are as popular as

A part of the annual fiesta in Pamplona is the running of fighting bulls through the streets, with young men testing their courage in the half-mile dash to the bull ring.

movie stars. They are featured in picture magazines and mobbed by admiring fans after the games.

Another popular sport is *pelota*, or jai alai. Originally a Basque game, the "fastest game in the world" is played on a large court known as a *frontón*, which is sometimes outdoors but more often is indoors and lighted. A player with a curving wicker basket (a *cesta*) attached to one wrist hurls a hard rubber ball against a concrete wall. The ball ricochets at great speed and must be caught by an opposing player, who then hurls it against the wall again. As in handball, the idea is to put the ball where the opposing players cannot reach it and thus win the point. Pelota has spread to Spanish-speaking countries of Central and South America and to the United States.

Other sports that have gained an enthusiastic following in Spain are cross-country cycling, golf, and tennis. Spain has produced international champions in all of these sports.

Bullfighting, for which Spaniards are so well known, is not considered a sport; it is art, a spectacle, and a Spanish tradition. In fact, Spaniards don't call it "bullfighting"—they call it a *corrida*, or "running of the bull."

A bullfight is performed by three *matadores* alternately fighting two bulls each. Each matador is assisted by a *cuadrilla*, a team of five men—two *picadores* and three *banderilleros*. In a sense, a bullfight is like a play with a set plot. The plot calls for the bull to die and the matador to emerge victorious. The essential feature of any performance is how well the mata-

Bullfighting is more than a sport in Spain; it is an art and a tradition.

dor completes the required, stylized movements. Like an aerial trapeze artist, he accepts the possibility of injury or even death at the hands of the powerful, 1,000-pound bull. He must also master his own fear, thereby proving that he possesses the quality Spaniards most admire—physical courage.

Each bullfight has three acts. In the first act, the picadores, mounted on horseback, dig a lance into the top of the bull's neck to weaken the animal's powerful tossing muscle and to make it angry. Next, the banderilleros plunge darts called *banderillas* into the bull's back. Finally, the matador maneuvers the tiring animal to a halt, steps in front of it, and kills it by driving a sword into its neck.

The bullfight season in Spain runs from the end of March through October. Madrid's Plaza de Toros, which seats 25,000, attracts the most famous bullfighters in Spain and stages some of the country's best fights during the San Isidro fair each May. Bullfights are also staged at most regional festivals during the season.

Although the popularity of bullfighting has decreased in recent years, thousands still crowd into the arenas on festival days. The big fights are televised across the country. Spaniards will stop what they are doing and push their way into lounges and restaurants to watch the spectacle. Good *toreadores* are held in high esteem and are awarded princely fees for a single corrida.

Art and Culture

When visitors to Madrid walk through the Prado—the National Museum of Painting and Sculpture—they find a brilliant cross section of the rich cultural heritage Spain has brought to the world. In the Prado are paintings by Diego Velázquez (1599–1660), who portrayed the personalities of the court officials of his day with brilliant colors; Bartholomé Esteban Murillo (1617–1682), whose religious paintings had a soft, spiritual quality; and Francisco de Goya (1746–1828), who depicted man's inhumanity to man in a distinctive style that used free brushwork and brilliant colors. Goya

This world-famous painting by Pablo Picasso, "Guernica," was returned to the Prado in Madrid in 1981.

ranks as one of the first masters of modern art. One entire room in the Prado is set aside for two of his paintings that portray a Spanish uprising against the French in 1808.

Perhaps the greatest "Spanish" painter of all was El Greco (1541–1614). El Greco (whose name means "The Greek") was born in Greece, not Spain; however, he spent most of his career in Spain. Critics say that El Greco's paintings reflect the mysticism and religious emotionalism of Spain better than those of any native-born Spaniard.

Spain's most renowned 20th-century artist was Pablo Picasso (1881–1973), whose unorthodox images expressed the complexity of a rapidly changing world. In 1981, Picasso's "Guernica" was brought back to Spain after having been in New York City for years. Its arrival in Madrid was the highlight of that year's celebration of the hundredth anniversary of the artist's birth. This huge depiction of the horrors of war is now housed in an annex of the Prado.

Several other well-known 20th-century artists worked or were born in Spain. They include Salvador Dali, Juan Gris, and Joan Miró. Spanish sculptors, too, have a proud heritage. In earlier times they decorated the great cathedrals with religious figures in stone and wood. Today, sculptors create not just for churches, but for municipal projects such as city streets and parks as well.

Literature

Spanish literature is known for its realism, humor, and popular appeal. Many Spanish authors write for and about the common people, with popular themes of human dignity, pride, bravery, and honor.

The most popular type of fiction during medieval times was the novel of romantic chivalry, which told of brave knights who fought duels and performed other deeds of honor for the women they loved. An early example of this type of literature is *Amadís de Gaula*, by Garci Rodriguez de Montalvo, published in 1508.

Between 1530 and 1680—during Spain's Golden Age of exploration, intellectual life, and artistry—there was a flowering of Spanish literature. In the early 1600s, Miguel de Cervantes Saavedra (1547–1616), Spain's most celebrated author, published *Don Quixote de la Mancha*, a satire about Spain's chivalrous knights. *Don Quixote* is the story of a simple-minded man who believes he is a knight and sets out with his faithful companion, Sancho Panza, to right the wrongs of the world. Through the interplay of dialogue between these two characters, Cervantes makes philosophical comments on his times. *Don Quixote* has been translated into more languages than any other novel, and critics have called Cervantes's story the finest ever written.

Spanish dramatists enjoyed a similar success. During the 1500s, Spanish playwrights such as Juan del Encina (1468–1529) and Bartholomé de Torres Naharro (1476–1531) wrote plays to amuse the aristocracy. In the mid-1500s, Lope de Rueda (1510–1565) brought drama to the common people, staging his plays in town squares and marketplaces instead of in the castles of the nobility. Juan de la Cueva (1543–1610), who based his plays on the nation's history and legends, did much to elevate Spanish drama into national theatre.

Perhaps Spain's best-known dramatist was Lope de Vega (1562–1635), who wrote hundreds of plays. It was said that he could write a new play in a single day. He himself said that many of his plays were performed four days after he got the idea to write them. Tirso de Molina (1580–1648) also excelled in the theatre; among his work is the first introduction into literature of the Don Juan legend in the 1634 drama *El Burlador de Sevilla (The Trickster of Seville)*.

In the mid-1800s, Spanish novelists, essayists, and playwrights turned to realistic themes that gave accurate portrayals of the difficult life of many Spaniards and the social problems of the country. By 1900, a group dubbed the "Generation of '98" sparked a literary renaissance. The group's most notable figure was José Ortega y Gasset (1883–1955), a philosopher whose essays on contemporary culture in the early 1900s had a strong influence on later writers. Successful younger colleagues included such 20th-century figures as the poet Juan Ramón Jiménez (1881–1958), who won the 1956 Nobel Prize for literature for his *Platero and I*, and Federico García Lorca (1898–1936), a poet and dramatist who drew much of his themes from Spanish folk tradition. García Lorca was internationally acclaimed for his gypsy ballads and poetic theatre, but his career was cut shot when he was executed by Nationalists during the Civil War.

Early in the 20th century, dramatist Jacinto Benavente (1866–1954) wrote plays notable for their realism and social commentary. In the post-civil war era, novelist Camilo José Cela (b. 1916) won recognition for *La Familia de Pascual Duarte* (1942) and *La Colmena* (*The Hive*, 1951). Benavente received the Nobel Prize for literature in 1922, Cela in 1989.

Music

The vitality and rhythm of Spanish music is known around the world. The main musical instruments include the guitar, tambourine, castanets, and *qaita* (Spanish bagpipes). The world-renowned concert artist Andres Segovia (1893–1986) helped elevate the guitar to importance as a solo instrument. Segovia was also a conductor, composer, and teacher; in 1949, he founded the Barcelona Orchestra.

Each region of Spain has its distinctive folk music and dances and takes pride in keeping these forms alive. The colorful *flamenco*, a passionate dance done to the accompaniment of a guitar and castanets, originated with the Gypsies of southern Spain and features fancy footwork, flowing arm movements, and finger-snapping. The *sardana*, a Catalonian dance, is performed by a group holding hands in a circle. Other dances include the *bolero, jota, fandango, zarabanda*, and *seguidilla*.

Music and dancing keep the mood lively at regional fiestas. Music festivals such as the one held each July in the beautiful gardens of the Generalife in Granada and the Madrid International Opera Festival attract music lovers from far away. Jazz, rock, and other contemporary types of music are popular with young Spaniards.

The Alhambra in Granada is a magnificent example of Moorish architecture.

Architecture

Spanish architecture bears testimony to the talents of the different cultures that have washed across the country throughout its history. A surprising number of the many remarkable structures built by the Romans has survived. Nearly every Spanish province has a remnant of Roman architecture. One outstanding example is the aqueduct at Segovia, constructed of huge blocks of granite. Another is the bridge at Alcantara, built by the Emperor Trajan in 106 A.D. to span the Tagus River.

Moorish architects created lavish palaces, mosques, and other buildings, characterized by decoration in carved stone, wood, mosaics, and tiles, that remain intact today. Granada's magnificent Alhambra covers 400,000 square feet, has 300 rooms, and is adorned with dozens of pools and fountains. The Generalife, the country residence for the kings of Granada, is widely admired for its gardens.

In the period after the Christian reconquest of Spain, Muslims remaining in the country produced what is called *Mudejar* architecture, which combined the Moorish and Christian styles and reflected Spain's wealth from the New World. Fine examples of this can be found in Seville and Toledo. In the 13th century, French Gothic architecture—characterized by vaulting, pointed arches, and a strong vertical quality—influenced the native Muslim tradition; splendid examples of the resulting tradition can be found in the cathedrals of Seville, Toledo, León, and Burgos.

Other examples of outstanding architecture abound. Castles are so numerous that they have given their name to an entire region at the heart of the peninsula—Castile. Some of Spain's many remaining castles have been restored and have been turned into *paradores* and *albergues*—comfortable state-owned inns that attract tourists. Palaces, monasteries, and public buildings are other interesting architectural specimens. Contemporary Spanish architecture reflects the modern building style of the rest of Europe, with skyscrapers and office buildings that exhibit simple straight lines and expanses of glass.

King Juan Carlos I has been a source of stability and legitimacy to Spain's democratic institutions.

Spain Today

The transition from dictatorship to democracy took place with no widespread internal or foreign opposition. After Franco's death, the Cortes passed political reform laws that permitted all parties to participate in democratic elections. In 1978, a completely new constitution replaced Franco's "fundamental laws," providing for a representative form of government and free elections. The new constitution ensured respect for the law, recognized the personal rights of individuals, and guaranteed freedom of religion. The constitution also ensured personal privacy and the safety of individuals within their homes. It provided for freedom of the press and speech, the education of children, the right to own property, and the right to strike. It lowered the voting age from 21 to 18, resulting in a larger proportion of young voters. Finally, it established the 17 autonomous communities that give the regions control over their own local affairs. As King Juan Carlos said when he addressed the Cortes after its post-Franco election of 1977, "Democracy has begun."

Spain's new constitution provided for a parliament of two chambers; the parliament's official name is the Cortes Generales. The Congress of Deputies (350 members) is elected by popular vote by the 50 provinces with the number of deputies for each province based on population. The second chamber, the Senate, has 208 elected members (four from each of the 47 peninsular provinces, 16 from the island provinces, and two from each of the North African territories, Ceuta and Melilla) and another 46 designated by the parliaments of the autonomous regions.

The political party that elects the largest number (plurality) to the Congress of Deputies organizes the executive branch of the government for the succeeding four years. The leader of the successful party becomes prime minister, although he must be officially nominated by the monarch and approved by the Congress of Deputies.

Four years after the adoption of the 1978 constitution, Felipe González of the Socialist party became prime minister when his party won the general elections in a landslide. The Socialists took the next three elections as well, but with declining shares of the vote. In 1996, they gave way to the center-right Popular party, whose leader, José María Aznar, became prime minister. Like the last Socialist government, however, the Popular party controlled less than a majority of seats in the Cortes, and it needed the help of smaller parties to form a governing coalition.

The constitution of 1978 also provided for a new system of regional government based on 17 autonomous communities. Each autonomous community consists of several provinces with a common historical and cultural heritage. The communities are designed to give added authority and prestige to the regions and to meet the demands of separatists who have sought stronger regional self-government. Each province is governed by a delegation which varies in size from 24 to 51 members, elected from among the province's municipal officials. Each municipality, in turn, is governed by an elected municipal council, which selects one of its members to serve as mayor.

Recent national governments in Madrid have used the new constitution to try to solve some of the country's social problems. Because the Catholic church exercises much power in Spain (95 percent of all Spaniards practice the Roman Catholic religion), the government has sometimes been brought into opposition with the Catholic church over its use of the constitution. In 1981, for example, the Cortes voted to allow Spanish couples to divorce, an action which angered the church. The law now allows divorce by mutual consent after a two-year period of separation. There is also an ongoing controversy between church and state over the issue of abortion, a procedure to which the Catholic church is universally opposed. A 1985 ruling that legalized abortion in certain, limited cases was opposed by the church. An expanded law that was passed the next year, making abortion more widely available in private clinics, received continued church opposition. Church leaders were also angered when the Cortes passed legislation reducing criminal prosecution for the possession of small amounts of drugs (although penalties continued to be severe for drug dealers carrying large amounts).

Education

Since Spain's unification under the Christian kings in the 1400s, the Catholic church has run most of the schools. Educational reforms in the 1970s were designed to improve the quality of education, make it better suited to the industrialization of the country, and ensure that the educational system served all citizens fairly. The operation of most schools was turned over to the government. In 1984, the Cortes went further, giving the government the authority to monitor how public money was being spent on government, Catholic, and private schools.

Until a few decades ago, children of middle- and upper-class families were usually the only ones who could continue their education past the elementary grades. Sons and daughters of workers and poor families often had to leave school at 10 or 11 years of age to help their parents earn a living. Spanish law now requires that children stay in school until age 16.

Elementary school, covering the ages of 6 to 12 years, provides basic education. Then students move on to four years of compulsory secondary education, during which they receive some vocational training. After age 16, if they decide to continue, students can pursue further secondary education either in academics or in vocational subjects. The final stage is advanced vocational training or university education.

Relatively few students enter a university. To do so they must take an orientation course during their 12th school year that gives them additional courses of study and teaches them good study habits. When they reach the university, students choose between a technical school and the traditional "faculty" that includes history, philosophy, and languages. Three years of study earns a *diplomado*, the basic college degree. Two more years of

Recent governmental rulings on marital and educational matters have brought conflict with the Catholic church. Symbolized by this massive cathedral in Seville, the church dominated Spain's cultural and political life for centuries.

specialized study earns a *licenciado*—the equivalent of a master's degree in law, engineering, architecture, or another profession. Two additional years of study and research earns the student an advanced *doctorado* degree.

Spain has some of the oldest universities in Europe. The University of Salamanca was founded in the 13th century, as were the universities of

Valencia and Valladolid. The University of Barcelona was founded in the 15th century and the University of Madrid in the 16th century.

Health and Welfare

Health care in Spain has improved dramatically in recent decades. The number of physicians—41 per 10,000 inhabitants—is relatively high among western European countries. So are the life expectancies, 75 years for males and 82 years for females (both significantly higher than in the United States). The infant mortality rate, at roughly 6 deaths per 1,000 live births, is fairly typical for western Europe.

Workers at the lower income levels are provided with full medical and dental care, hospitalization, and medication at little or no cost. Other workers contribute a small part of their wages to a compulsory health insurance program to which their employer contributes about five times as much. A worker who is absent from work because of illness receives 75 percent of his wages for 24 months and full hospitalization for up to 18 months. Maternity leave grants 75 percent of the mother's wages for up to six weeks before and after birth.

Public health services are administered by all levels of government. The government provides direct health services to many people through health centers, general hospitals, maternity centers, children's hospitals, and psychiatric units. There are also a number of hospitals run by private institutions, churches, and the Red Cross. City hospitals have recently had difficulty caring for the increasing numbers of patients, many of whom are recent arrivals from rural areas.

Medical care is more limited in rural areas than in cities. Graduates of medical schools are supposed to spend a year practicing in a rural village before taking a position in a city, but many have avoided this duty. Village pharmacists often provide medical advice, and sometimes the government will send an instructor to a village to teach hygiene and child care.

A social security system protects all those who work, providing benefits to the unemployed, the disabled, and the retired. Social security is financed by contributions from all workers, employers, and the government.

Communications

Under Franco, newspapers and magazines were subject to censorship by the government, while television, radio, and motion pictures were operated by the government. The 1978 constitution guarantees freedom of expression, and newspapers and magazines are now free to publish the news they gather and to criticize the government.

More than 150 daily newspapers are published in Spain, and on a typical day about 25 percent of the country's citizens read a daily paper. The dailies with the largest circulations are based in Madrid and Barcelona. Madrid's *El País* is a highly respected paper that sells over 400,000 copies a day—and a million on Sundays. *ABC*, also based in Madrid, averages over 330,000 copies sold per day. The largest Barcelona newspapers are *La Vanguardia* and *El Periódico de Cataluña*, both averaging over 185,000 copies. Newspapers from other regions are also important. For example, the Basque Country's *El Pueblo Vasco* distributes more than 130,000 copies a day.

Spaniards also buy thousands of different weekly newspapers and magazines, including news magazines and economic journals. One popular type of magazine, called "Prensa del Corazon" (literally, "Press of the Heart"), highlights popular events and movie star gossip.

The number of television sets in Spain has increased rapidly in recent years, passing 16 million. From 1956 to 1990, the national government held a television monopoly; it established and controlled two national TV networks and nine regional ones. Now, though, the doors are open to private television companies as well. Not surprisingly, Spaniards favor the same kinds of programs as other Europeans. Many prime-time broadcasts offer sports, game shows, or TV movies.

There are 12 million radios in Spain, one for every three inhabitants, and they reach well over 40 percent of the population. As with television, the national government shares broadcasting privileges with private groups. The government network, called Radio Nacional de España, has the largest budget and number of stations, though not the greatest audience. A number of the regional and municipal governments also have their own radio outlets, as do church organizations.

Transportation

Many more Spaniards own autos now than a few decades ago. Some 13.4 million passenger cars now roll across the Spanish countryside, joined by 2.9 million commercial vehicles. In 1963, by contrast, there were only 529,000 passenger cars and 260,000 commercial vehicles.

The country's highway system has scarcely kept pace with the increasing number of motor vehicles. Most highways radiate from Madrid, which makes it difficult to drive from north to south or east to west or travel from one region to another. Spain has only 204,000 miles of paved highway—only 1,700 miles of this is superhighway. Traffic often backs up on the secondary, two-lane roads.

Trucks add to the highway crowding. Much of the country's freight is transported by truck, although quantities of long-range bulk cargoes such as coal are carried by freight trains. To satisfy the Spanish craving for fresh fish, trucks load up at one of several seaports and drive all night to bring the seafood inland to city restaurants.

Traffic jams in the cities are reported to be some of the worst in Europe. One of the causes of this problem is the Spanish tradition of returning home in the middle of the day to have dinner with the family. The result is that there are usually four traffic jams instead of the two that are common in countries where workers eat their lunch close to the worksite.

More than 8,800 miles of railroad tracks carry trains throughout Spain. The rail system provides fewer railroads per square mile than many other European nations, and most of the rail lines, like the highways, radiate from Madrid. One notable train is the "Talgo," a fast, streamlined train that runs 780 miles from Madrid to Paris. Clever engineers have installed features that make the train unique: The Talgo express can adjust the width of its axles when it crosses the border from Spain to France—a necessity, because Spanish railways have tracks that are more widely spaced than those of the rest of Europe.

Within cities, it is often easiest to bypass rush-hour traffic by using mass transportation. Three cities—Madrid, Barcelona, and Seville—have metropolitan subway networks.

There are 96 airports in Spain, the most heavily used of which are in Madrid, Palma de Mallorca in the Balearic Islands, and Barcelona. Iberia Airlines, Europe's third-busiest airline, is owned and operated by the Spanish government. Iberia connects cities within Spain and flies to many western European cities, as well as to North and South America. Another national airline, AVIACO, flies passengers mainly to cities and towns within Spain.

In Madrid, primitive, hutlike homes are being rapidly replaced by modern apartment buildings.

Spain and the Future

Despite a recent history of isolation, Spain no longer stands apart from the rest of Europe. Spaniards may continue to look inward at their regional origins, but they are increasingly looking outward toward Europe and the rest of the world.

Democracy has replaced dictatorship in the political life of the country. Repressive measures such as censorship of the press and one-party rule are gone, if not entirely forgotten. In their place, Spaniards enjoy universal suffrage and vigorous competition between political parties that represent differing points of view.

Spain's new democratic climate was tested in 1981, when renegade officers of the Civil Guard—Spain's national police force—forced their way into the Congress of Deputies in Madrid and took most of the country's leaders hostage. King Juan Carlos I responded calmly to the emergency, negotiating a peaceful surrender of the rebels and avoiding any bloodshed. The outcome of this potentially disastrous incident reflected a growing political maturity. Instead of resorting to force of arms, the king acted in a restrained way, preventing the rebel army officers from overthrowing the new democracy. This event was also significant because it signaled that the people of Spain were less concerned with the philosophy of a particular political party than they were with the overall health of their country.

Since 1975, Spain has turned increasingly from an economy that is planned and directed by the central government to one in which individual businesspeople make economic decisions based on the supply and demand of the marketplace. Now that Spain has become a member of the European Union, its products compete in European and world markets with the products of other countries. This new competitiveness has brought hard times to some traditional industries, such as agriculture and coal mining, but it has opened up bright opportunities in others. Foreign

In 1981, renegade officers of the Civil Guard forced their way into the Spanish parliament and took most of the country's leaders hostage. Here Colonel Antonio Tejero de Molina, leader of the takeover, brandishes a pistol on the podium.

companies, invited to participate in joint ventures with Spanish firms, share their technological know-how and organizational ability with their Spanish partners, and both share in the resulting profits. The turnaround in the economy has created new jobs, enabling many workers who left to find work in neighboring countries or in Latin America to return home.

Spain's traditional isolation has broken down as its people have adopted many of the ways of Europe. An increase in the number of tourists has added to this Europeanization of the country. Spain has opened the door wide to these visitors, converting unused castles into popular *paradores* (government-operated inns) and building contemporary resorts to encourage the flow.

Spain's leaders hope that the boom in tourism will offset the country's other economic problems. Poor soil, the lack of rainfall over much of the country, and the inefficient size of small northern farms all contribute to low rates of production, scant farm income, and job scarcity in agriculture. In the south, the concentration of land in the hands of a few wealthy families provides little incentive for ambitious young people who might like to earn their living from the land instead of in a factory.

The Spaniard has always admired those who attain great things through their individual efforts—the artist, the saint, the poet, the conquistador. It remains to be seen if he can now submerge his strong tendency to be an individualist—to go his own way no matter what others may want—in the best interests of the nation as a whole. He will also have to keep his love for his own region and its ways within reasonable limits. Through the country's turbulent history, regions have fiercely preserved many of their

With the coming of democracy demonstrations for women's liberation were allowed.

privileges and customs. Catalonians, for example, insist on speaking their own language even though most Spaniards don't understand it; and the Basque separatist groups continue to commit terrorist acts in their fight for a Basque nation in northern Spain and southern France.

But if the individualism of the average Spaniard tends to pull the country apart, other factors hold it together: the unifying influence of the monarchy, the need for business to pull together in the face of European competition, and the functioning democratic system of government. As a member of the European community, Spain brings with it a proud history as a world power and a brilliant cultural heritage that has earned the world's admiration. Brighter days seem assured for Spain and its people as it once again plays a prominent role on the world stage.

‹GLOSSARY›

Alcalde   An administrative or judicial officer of a village, town, or district.

Alcázar   A fortified castle.

Caudillo   A military leader, usually a leader of guerrilla or irregular forces who are loyal to him personally. During the Spanish Civil War, the term was applied by the Nationalists to General Francisco Franco.

Conquistador   A leader in the Spanish conquest of the Americas.

Corrida   A bullfight; literally, a "running of the bulls."

Las Cortes   The Cortes Generales, the Spanish parliament, which consists of the Congress of Deputies and the Senate.

España   The Spanish word for "Spain."

Fiesta   A festival. Fiestas, often inspired by religious holidays, feature music, street dancing, regional dishes and drinks—and occasionally a bullfight.

Hidalgo; Infanzón   Knights who fought for the Christian reconquest of Spain.

Latifundio   A large estate in southern Spain.

Matador   A Spanish bullfighter.

Meseta   The high, dry plateau that covers the central part of Spain.

Mudejar   The architectural style produced by Muslims remaining in Spain following the Christian reconquest.

Moors   Muslims from North Africa who invaded and conquered Spain in the early 8th century.

Parador   A government-owned inn located in a restored castle, mansion, or monastery that offers tourists unique overnight accommodations.

Paseo   An evening stroll or promenade. In this traditional Spanish custom, people of all ages step out on the street to walk and chat with friends and neighbors.

Pelota   A fast-moving game originated by the Basques, played with a rubber ball that is hurled at great speed against a wall. Pelota is played in an arena called a *fronton*. The game is also called *jai alai*.

Peseta   The Spanish unit of currency.

Plaza Major   The main square of a typical town in Spain. In most cases, the square is bordered by a covered arcade.

Reconquista   The seven-century Christian reconquest of Spain, after it fell to the Moors in the 8th century.

Spanish Armada   A fleet of 130 ships sent by King Philip II of Spain to clear the path for his army to invade England in 1588. Its defeat was one of the most decisive battles in European history.

Tasca   A small tavern.

Tertulia   A café gathering, often at a regular time and place, in which friends gather to chat, eat, and enjoy each other's company. In earlier times, tertulias often centered on a well-known literary or artistic figure.

◄INDEX►